Mastermind Python:
From Logic to Application

A Practical Guide to Mastering Python Programming

Dr. Deepak Kumar Sharma

Copyright © <2024> <Deepak Kumar Sharma>

Made with ❤ on the Notion Press Platform

www.notionpress.com

This book is dedicated to my students, whose insatiable curiosity and relentless pursuit of knowledge continually inspire me. Your passion for learning and your drive to challenge yourselves are the reasons I strive to be a better educator every day.

To my colleagues and mentors, thank you for your constant support, guidance, and encouragement throughout my journey. Your wisdom has shaped my thinking and pushed me to excel both as a teacher and a learner.

To my family, whose love and understanding have been my foundation, I am forever grateful. You have been my greatest source of strength, offering me unwavering support in both my professional and personal endeavors.

Lastly, to all aspiring programmers, this book is for you. May it ignite the spark of curiosity, foster critical thinking, and empower you to master Python and use it to create, innovate, and shape the future

Contents

Foreword

In the rapidly evolving world of technology, Python has become one of the most versatile and in-demand programming languages. Whether you're developing web applications, diving into data analysis, or exploring machine learning, Python's simplicity and power make it the language of choice for developers worldwide. Dr. Deepak Kumar Sharma's **"Mastermind Python: From Logic to Application"** is a timely and invaluable resource for anyone looking to master this essential tool.

Dr. Sharma is not only a distinguished academic but also a seasoned practitioner of Python programming. With over 12 years of experience in teaching, research, and hands-on application, he has established himself as a thought leader in the field. His ability to translate complex concepts into clear, practical lessons makes this book a must-have for aspiring and experienced programmers alike.

What sets this book apart is its comprehensive approach, taking the reader on a journey from the foundational logic of Python to its real-world applications. Dr. Sharma emphasizes not just the "how" of coding, but the "why," helping readers develop a deeper understanding of Python's principles and capabilities. Through carefully crafted examples and exercises, this book ensures that learners not only write code but write effective, efficient, and scalable code.

With a strong academic background and a proven track record in training several professionals, Dr. Sharma's insights offer a rare blend of theoretical depth and practical expertise. **"Mastermind Python"** is more than just a textbook—it's a guide to becoming a true Python expert, equipping you with the tools to tackle challenges in real-world projects.

As you explore the pages of this book, you'll find yourself not just learning Python but mastering it. Whether you're a beginner or looking to deepen your knowledge, **"Mastermind Python: From Logic to Application"** is the perfect companion on your programming journey.

Dr. Deepak Kumar Sharma

Date: 25 Nov 2024

Preface

The journey of writing "Mastermind Python: From Logic to Application" has been both an exciting and deeply rewarding experience for me. As an educator with over 12 years of experience in teaching and training Python to thousands of students and professionals, I've witnessed firsthand the transformative power of programming. Python, with its simplicity, versatility, and efficiency, has become the language of choice for many aspiring developers, and I am thrilled to share my insights and experiences in this book.

The idea for this book emerged from my passion for teaching and my desire to make Python more accessible to learners at all levels. Over the years, I've seen many students struggle to understand the core concepts of programming, and I realized that many textbooks are either too technical or not comprehensive enough to bridge the gap between theory and real-world application. With this book, I aim to provide a clear, practical guide that takes readers from the basics of Python to its powerful applications in various domains.

"Mastermind Python" is not just about writing code; it's about understanding the logic behind it. It's about mastering the thought process that turns an idea into a working solution. This book takes you through Python's fundamental concepts like data structures, object-oriented programming, and algorithms, while also offering practical applications that you can use in your own projects. Whether you're a beginner starting your coding journey or someone looking to refine your Python skills, this book is designed to help you grow as a programmer.

The path to writing this book was a journey of reflection, learning, and rethinking how I teach Python. My goal has always been to make learning interactive and impactful. Through numerous workshops, courses, and faculty development programs, I've refined the approach that's embodied in this book: active learning, hands-on coding, and an emphasis on problem-solving. The exercises and examples in this book are designed to encourage you to not just read but also actively engage with the content and solve problems using Python.

I hope this book inspires you to not only learn Python but to also think critically and creatively as you embark on your journey in programming. Python is a tool—one that, when mastered, can open countless doors in the world of software development, data science, automation, and beyond. My wish is for you to take what you learn from this book and use it to build solutions that make a difference in your world.

Thank you for choosing this book as your guide to mastering Python. I am confident that it will be a valuable resource on your programming journey.

Dr. Deepak Kumar Sharma

25 Nov 2024

Acknowledgments

Writing this book has been a rewarding journey, and I would like to take this opportunity to express my heartfelt gratitude to those who supported me throughout this endeavor.

First and foremost, I would like to thank my family for their unwavering support and encouragement. To my parents, for their constant belief in my potential and for always inspiring me to pursue my dreams. To my wife, **Ms. Swati Sharma**, and children, **Shivansh Sharma** and **Dhruvika Sharma**, for their patience and understanding during the countless hours spent writing and revising this book—your love and support have been my rock.

I am deeply grateful to my colleagues for their continuous guidance and intellectual stimulation. Special thanks to my friends who have shared their insights and experiences with me over the years. Your feedback and constructive criticism have helped me grow both as a teacher and a writer.

I would also like to acknowledge my students, past and present, whose enthusiasm and curiosity have been a constant source of inspiration. Your dedication to learning Python and your passion for technology motivated me to share my knowledge in this book. You are the true reason I continue to teach and improve every day.

Finally, I would like to express my gratitude to all the Python enthusiasts, educators, and developers whose work in the field continues to inspire and drive innovation. Your contributions have helped make Python the powerful tool it is today.

Thank you all for your support, encouragement, and belief in me. This book would not have been possible without each of you.

Introduction

Welcome to *Mastermind Python: From Logic to Application*! This book is designed to provide you with a structured and in-depth exploration of Python, from the very basics to its application in solving real-world problems. Whether you're just starting out or looking to enhance your existing Python knowledge, this book will serve as a comprehensive guide to mastering Python.

Insights from the Book:

- **Building Strong Foundations**: The first few chapters introduce the essential concepts of Python, including its history, key features, and basic syntax. You'll learn about data types, operators, and how Python handles input and output operations, setting the groundwork for more advanced topics.

- **Control Flow and Loops**: As you progress, the book delves into Python's control flow mechanisms, such as conditional statements (if-else) and loops (for, while). These foundational constructs are essential for building logic in your programs and solving problems efficiently.

- **Functions and Modular Programming**: The concept of functions is explored in detail, where you'll learn how to define functions, use parameters, and return values. You'll also understand the importance of modular programming for writing clean, reusable code.

- **Data Structures**: A key focus of the book is on Python's powerful built-in data structures, including lists, tuples, sets, and dictionaries. You'll explore how to create, access, and manipulate these structures, which are crucial for managing and organizing data in Python programs.

- **Exception Handling**: Handling errors and exceptions is a vital skill in programming. This book covers Python's exception-handling mechanisms, teaching you how to write robust and fault-tolerant programs.

- **Object-Oriented Programming (OOP)**: The book delves into Object-Oriented Programming concepts such as classes, objects, inheritance, and polymorphism. By understanding these principles, you'll learn how to model real-world entities in your Python programs effectively.

- **Application Building**: Towards the end, the book emphasizes putting your knowledge into practice. You'll explore real-world scenarios and examples, building Python applications with the core concepts covered throughout the chapters.

Each chapter is equipped with exercises and logic-check questions to test your understanding and reinforce the concepts. By the end of this book, you'll have mastered Python's fundamentals and be well-equipped to apply your knowledge in various contexts, including solving complex problems, automating tasks, and much more.

Get ready to embark on a learning journey where logic meets application, and become a Python mastermind!

1. Python Introduction

1.1 Overview of Python

Python is a versatile, high-level programming language famous for its simplicity and readability. It was created by Guido van Rossum and first introduced to the world in 1991. Python's foundational philosophy revolves around making code easy to read and write, ensuring it is accessible to both novice programmers and experienced developers. This focus on user-friendliness, combined with its powerful capabilities, has cemented Python as one of the most widely-used programming languages globally.

Unlike many other programming languages, Python supports multiple programming paradigms. These include:

i. Procedural programming, which focuses on sequentially executed instructions.

ii. Object-oriented programming, which organizes code into reusable objects.

iii. Functional programming, which emphasizes the use of functions as the primary building blocks for code.

By offering such flexibility, Python enables developers to adapt it to a wide variety of use cases, ranging from simple automation tasks to complex scientific computations.

1.2 History and Development

Python's journey began in the late 1980s when Guido van Rossum sought to create a language that was both easy to use and powerful enough for real-world applications. The language drew inspiration from the ABC programming language, which was developed to teach programming concepts effectively.

The first public release of Python occurred in 1991. Since then, the language has evolved significantly:

i. Python 2.0 (released in 2000): This version introduced several important features, such as list comprehensions, which make it easier to process collections of data, and garbage collection, which automates memory management. Python 2 became popular but also carried certain design limitations.

ii. Python 3.0 (released in 2008): This version marked a major overhaul of the language. It aimed to eliminate inconsistencies and improve usability, but it wasn't backward-compatible with Python 2. Python 3 introduced better support for Unicode, improved data structures, and removed redundant features.

The decision to create a non-compatible version ensured Python's long-term sustainability, even though it required developers to transition their codebases over time.

1.3 Why Python?

Python's popularity stems from its simplicity, versatility, and widespread adoption across industries. Below are the key reasons that explain why Python is a preferred language for many developers and organizations:

1. Readability and Simplicity

Python uses indentation to define code blocks instead of curly braces or keywords. This ensures that Python code is clean and easy to follow, even for those new to programming. Python follows the principle that "There should be one—and preferably only one—obvious way to do it." This consistency makes the language intuitive and easy to maintain, even for large, complex projects.

2. Versatility

Python accommodates diverse programming styles, such as procedural, object-oriented, and functional programming. This adaptability allows developers to choose the most suitable approach for their tasks. Python boasts a rich ecosystem of libraries and frameworks, which significantly reduce development time. Examples include:

- NumPy and pandas for data analysis.

- Django and Flask for web development.

- TensorFlow and PyTorch for machine learning and artificial intelligence.

These tools extend Python's capabilities and make it a powerful choice for specialized domains.

3. Ease of Learning

Python is often recommended as the first programming language for beginners due to its clear syntax and straightforward concepts. Its gentle learning curve allows newcomers to focus on problem-solving rather than syntax intricacies. Python has extensive documentation, tutorials, and community-created resources that cater to learners at every level. This wealth of material helps beginners start quickly while providing advanced developers with opportunities for deeper learning.

4. Community and Ecosystem

Python has a large, vibrant community that actively contributes to the language's development. Platforms like Stack Overflow, GitHub, and Python forums provide support for developers of all skill levels. Python is open-source software, meaning its source code is freely available for anyone to use, modify, or distribute. This openness has fostered innovation and collaboration on a global scale.

5. Cross-Platform Compatibility

Python is designed to run on multiple operating systems, such as Windows, macOS, and Linux, without requiring modifications. This cross-platform compatibility makes Python an excellent choice for projects intended to operate in diverse environments. Python interpreters are readily available on almost every system, allowing developers to execute their code in environments ranging from powerful cloud servers to small embedded devices.

6. Productivity and Speed

Python's simplicity allows developers to write concise code that accomplishes more with fewer lines. Combined with its rich libraries, Python enables faster prototyping and development cycles. Python integrates well with other programming languages, enabling developers to call C/C++ functions, use Java libraries via Jython, or work with .NET components through IronPython. This makes Python a versatile tool for complex, multi-language projects.

7. Performance and Efficiency

Python handles memory allocation and deallocation automatically through garbage collection, which reduces the likelihood of memory leaks and enhances efficiency. Although Python is not inherently the fastest language, its performance can be significantly enhanced using tools like Cython, Numba, and PyPy. These tools allow developers to optimize specific portions of code without sacrificing Python's simplicity.

8. Industry Adoption and Job Market

Python is extensively used across various industries, including web development, data science, finance, education, and healthcare. Its adaptability makes it a reliable choice for everything from small scripts to large-scale enterprise applications. With the rise of data science, machine learning, and artificial intelligence, Python skills are in high demand. Mastering Python can lead to lucrative career opportunities and open doors to exciting projects.

Python's unique combination of simplicity, flexibility, and power has positioned it as a dominant language in the programming world. Whether you're a beginner taking your first steps into coding or a professional building advanced system, Python offers a reliable and rewarding platform to achieve your goals.

1.4 Features of Python

Python stands out as a programming language due to its combination of simplicity, flexibility, and power. One of its defining characteristics is its ease of use, which makes it an ideal language for both beginners and experienced developers. Its syntax is straightforward and closely resembles the English language, making it intuitive and easy to learn. This simplicity significantly lowers the barrier to entry for new programmers, allowing them to quickly start writing functional and meaningful code.

As an interpreted language, Python processes code line by line, which offers several advantages. For one, it simplifies debugging by allowing developers to identify and fix errors during runtime without the need for lengthy compilation processes. Additionally, this feature makes Python inherently portable, enabling the same code to run seamlessly across multiple operating systems, such as Windows, macOS, and Linux, without requiring modifications.

Python's support for object-oriented programming (OOP) is another feature that enhances its versatility. OOP allows developers to create reusable and modular code by organizing it into classes and objects. This structure promotes better code organization, encapsulation, and reusability, which is especially beneficial in larger projects where clarity and maintainability are essential.

A significant advantage of Python is its extensive standard library, which comes preloaded with modules and packages designed to handle a wide range of tasks. Whether you are working on file manipulation, system-level operations, web development, or data analysis, Python's standard library provides ready-to-use tools that save developers from reinventing the wheel. This rich ecosystem not only accelerates development but also allows developers to focus on solving specific problems rather than spending time on foundational coding tasks.

Python is dynamically typed, meaning that developers do not need to declare the type of a variable explicitly. Instead, the type is determined during runtime. This feature simplifies coding and reduces boilerplate, making the language more concise and readable. However, it also requires developers to exercise caution to avoid potential errors arising from unexpected type changes.

The language's cross-platform compatibility is another strength. Python programs can run on any operating system that has the Python interpreter installed, ensuring flexibility and reducing dependency on specific hardware or software environments. This feature makes Python an attractive choice for developing portable applications that can cater to a broad audience.

Finally, Python's success is bolstered by its strong and active community. This community not only drives the language's development but also provides extensive support through forums, tutorials, documentation, and open-source contributions. Whether you are a beginner looking for guidance or an expert tackling advanced challenges, Python's community offers a wealth of resources and support that ensure a smooth development experience.

In summary, Python's features—its simplicity, interpreted nature, object-oriented support, extensive library, dynamic typing, cross-platform compatibility, and robust community—make it a language that is not only easy to learn but also highly adaptable for a wide variety of applications.

1.5 Python Use Cases

Python's adaptability and rich ecosystem of libraries make it one of the most versatile programming languages, enabling its application across numerous domains. Here are some key areas where Python plays a significant role:

Web Development

Python is widely used in web development, where frameworks like Django and Flask provide a robust foundation for creating dynamic and scalable web applications. Django, known for its "batteries included" approach, comes with built-in features such as authentication, database management, and URL routing, allowing developers to build secure and high-performance web applications with ease. Flask, on the other hand, offers a lightweight and flexible framework, making it ideal for smaller projects or when customization is a priority. These frameworks, along with Python's readability and efficiency, make Python a preferred language for web developers.

Data Science and Machine Learning

Python has become synonymous with data science and machine learning due to its extensive collection of specialized libraries and tools. Libraries like NumPy and pandas are essential for numerical computing and data manipulation, allowing scientists to handle large datasets efficiently. For data visualization, tools such as Matplotlib and Seaborn enable the creation of insightful charts and graphs. In machine learning, libraries like Scikit-learn, TensorFlow, and PyTorch provide powerful frameworks for building, training, and deploying machine learning models. Python's simplicity and the active development of these libraries make it the go-to language for solving complex data-driven problems.

Automation and Scripting

Python excels in automating repetitive and mundane tasks, making it a favorite among IT professionals and system administrators. Its simple syntax and readability enable the development of scripts for a wide range of tasks, such as file organization, data extraction, and system monitoring. Libraries like Selenium and BeautifulSoup extend Python's capabilities to web automation and web scraping, allowing users to interact with websites programmatically or extract large amounts of data from online sources efficiently.

Scientific Computing

Python's role in scientific computing has grown significantly due to its specialized libraries designed for research and academia. SciPy offers tools for advanced numerical computations, such as optimization, integration, and signal processing, while SymPy is a symbolic mathematics library capable of algebraic computation and solving equations symbolically. Python's ability to handle complex mathematical operations and simulate scientific models has made it indispensable in fields like physics, biology, and engineering research.

Game Development

Python's utility extends to game development, where libraries like Pygame simplify the process of creating games and multimedia applications. Pygame provides modules for handling graphics, sound, and input devices, enabling developers to build 2D games quickly. While Python is not commonly used for high-end game development, it serves as an excellent tool for prototyping game ideas, educational projects, and creating simple yet engaging games.

Python's versatility continues to expand its relevance across industries, from building websites and analyzing data to automating workflows and conducting scientific research. Its accessibility, combined with a thriving ecosystem of libraries and frameworks, makes Python an indispensable tool for professionals and enthusiasts alike.

1.6 Installing Python

Python can be installed on various operating systems, and the process slightly differs based on the platform. Below are step-by-step instructions for installing Python on Windows, macOS, and Linux.

Installing Python on Windows

To install Python on a Windows system, follow these steps:

a. Download the latest Python installer from the official Python website at https://www.python.org/.

b. Run the installer. During the installation process, ensure you check the box labeled "Add Python to PATH." This step is crucial as it allows you to run Python directly from the command prompt without additional configuration.

c. Follow the on-screen prompts to complete the installation. Once installed, you can verify the installation by opening the command prompt and typing:

python --version

This command will display the installed version of Python.

Installing Python on macOS

Although macOS comes with Python pre-installed, the version included is often outdated. It is recommended to install the latest version for development purposes.

a. Install Homebrew, a popular package manager for macOS. Open the Terminal application and run the following command:

/bin/bash -c "$(curl -fsSL https://raw.githubusercontent.com/Homebrew/install/HEAD/install.sh)"

b. Once Homebrew is installed, use it to install Python by running:

brew install python

c. After the installation, you can verify the installed version of Python by typing:

python3 --version

Installing Python on Linux

Most Linux distributions, such as Ubuntu and Fedora, come with Python pre-installed. However, it may not be the latest version. To install or update Python, follow these steps:

a. Update the package manager by running the following command in the terminal:

sudo apt-get update

b. Install Python using the package manager:

sudo apt-get install python3

c. After installation, check the installed version by typing:

python3 --version

1.7 Writing Your First Python Program

To get started with Python, we will write a simple "Hello, World!!!" program.

1. Open your preferred text editor or an Integrated Development Environment (IDE) like PyCharm or Visual Studio Code.
2. Type the following code:

print("Hello, World!!!")

3. Save the file with a **.py** extension, for example, **hello.py**.
4. Open a terminal or command prompt, navigate to the directory where you saved the file, and run the program using the command:

python hello.py

You should see the output:

Hello, World!!!

1.8 Interactive Mode and Scripting Mode in Python

Python comes with an Integrated Development and Learning Environment (IDLE), a user-friendly tool that provides two primary modes of operation: Interactive Mode and Scripting Mode. These modes cater to different needs, from learning and testing small pieces of code to developing complete applications. This section explores both modes in detail.

Interactive Mode in Python IDLE

Interactive Mode allows users to enter Python commands one at a time and see immediate results. This mode is especially beneficial for beginners and for tasks that require quick feedback, such as testing code snippets and debugging.

Key Features of Interactive Mode

a. Immediate Feedback: Commands entered in the Python Shell are executed immediately, and the output is displayed in real-time.
b. REPL Environment: IDLE functions as a REPL (Read-Eval-Print Loop), where it reads input, evaluates it, prints the result, and waits for the next command.
c. Ease of Use: The graphical interface includes features such as syntax highlighting, autocomplete, and error highlighting, making it accessible for learners.

How to Access Interactive Mode

a. Open IDLE from the Start menu (e.g., "IDLE (Python 3.x 64-bit)").
b. The Python Shell window appears, indicated by the >>> prompt, where you can start entering commands.

Example
In the Python Shell, type:

```
print("Hello, Interactive Mode!")
```

The output will be displayed immediately:

```
Hello, Interactive Mode!
```

Applications of Interactive Mode

a. Learning and Experimentation: Ideal for trying out Python syntax, functions, and libraries.
b. Debugging: Useful for testing small sections of code to identify and fix errors.
c. Prototyping: Allows quick creation and validation of small code snippets.

Scripting Mode in Python IDLE

Scripting Mode is designed for writing, saving, and executing Python programs stored in files. This mode is suitable for developing more complex and reusable code.

Key Features of Scripting Mode

a. Script Files: Python code is saved in .py files, which can be reused and organized.
b. Editor Window: IDLE provides an editor with features like syntax highlighting, automatic indentation, and line numbers, ensuring better readability and organization.
c. Batch Execution: Entire scripts can be executed at once, enabling the execution of comprehensive programs.

How to Use Scripting Mode

a. Create a New File: Open IDLE and select File > New File to open the editor window.
b. Write Code: Enter your Python code. For example:

```
# hello.py

print("Hello, Scripting Mode!")
```

c. Save the Script: Go to File > Save, choose a location, and save the file with a .py extension (e.g., hello.py).
d. Run the Script: Press F5 or select Run > Run Module. The output will appear in the Python Shell.

Applications of Scripting Mode

1. Application Development: Used for writing and managing larger programs, such as web or desktop applications.
2. Automation: Enables the creation of scripts for repetitive tasks, such as file handling or data processing.
3. Scheduled Tasks: Scripts can be executed at specified times using task scheduling tools like Windows Task Scheduler.

1.9 Exercise Questions

1) Who created Python, and when was it first introduced?
Ans. Guido van Rossum created Python, and it was first introduced in 1991.

2) Name the three primary programming paradigms supported by Python. Provide a brief description of each.
Ans.
a) Procedural programming: Focuses on sequentially executed instructions.
b) Object-oriented programming: Organizes code into reusable objects.
c) Functional programming: Emphasizes the use of functions as the primary building blocks for code.

3) How does Python's foundational philosophy make it user-friendly for both novice and experienced developers?
Ans. Python's philosophy emphasizes code readability and simplicity, ensuring that programs are easy to write and understand. Its syntax is clear and intuitive, which reduces complexity for beginners and allows professionals to work efficiently.

4) What programming language inspired the creation of Python, and why was it used as a reference?
Ans. Python was inspired by the ABC programming language, which was designed to teach programming concepts effectively. It served as a reference for creating an easy-to-use yet powerful language.

5) Mention two major features introduced in Python 2.0 and two improvements made in Python 3.0.
Ans.
a) Python 2.0: Introduced list comprehensions and garbage collection.
b) Python 3.0: Provided better Unicode support and improved data structures.

6) Why was Python 3 designed to be backward-incompatible, and what were the benefits of this decision?

Ans. Python 3 was designed to eliminate inconsistencies and improve usability. Although it required developers to transition their codebases, it ensured the language's long-term sustainability.

7) List three reasons why Python is considered an excellent language for beginners.

Ans.

a) Its syntax is simple and similar to English.

b) It has extensive resources like documentation and tutorials.

c) It uses indentation instead of complex symbols, which makes code easy to read.

8) Explain how Python's cross-platform compatibility benefits developers.

Ans. Python can run on various operating systems (Windows, macOS, Linux) without modification, enabling developers to create portable applications that function in diverse environments.

9) What is the advantage of Python being dynamically typed, and what caution must developers take when using this feature?

Ans. Dynamic typing allows variables to change types during runtime, simplifying coding and reducing boilerplate. Developers must be cautious about unexpected type changes, which can cause runtime errors.

10) Describe two key features of Python's standard library that make it convenient for developers.

Ans.

a) It includes modules for tasks like file manipulation, system operations, and web development.

b) It provides ready-to-use tools, reducing development time and effort.

2. Basics in Python

This chapter covers the fundamental aspects of Python, including data types, tokens, operators, input and output functions, and much more. As we explore each concept, we'll use examples that resonate with Indian culture, traditions, and everyday life to make the learning experience relatable and engaging.

2.1 Data Types in Python

Data types are a crucial part of any programming language, and Python is no exception. In Python, the type of a variable determines what kind of data it can store, such as numbers, text, or more complex structures. Let's explore the common data types in Python through examples that connect with our everyday experiences in India.

a) Numeric Data Types

Python supports three types of numeric data types:

i.   Integer (int): Represents whole numbers, both positive and negative, without any decimal point.

Example: Consider the number of mangoes in a basket during the summer season, which are whole numbers.

```python
mangoes_in_basket = 25
print(mangoes_in_basket, type(mangoes_in_basket))  # Output: 25 <class 'int'>
```

ii.   Float (float): Represents decimal numbers, such as the price of a kilogram of turmeric or the temperature in Celsius during a hot summer day.

```python
price_per_kg_turmeric = 200.75
print(price_per_kg_turmeric, type(price_per_kg_turmeric))  # Output: 200.75 <class 'float'>
```

iii. Complex (complex): Represents complex numbers, written in the form a + bj, where a is the real part and b is the imaginary part. Complex numbers are used in various engineering and scientific computations.

```python
complex_number = 3 + 4j
print(complex_number, type(complex_number))  # Output: (3+4j) <class 'complex'>
```

b) Text Data Type

i.   String (str): Represents a sequence of characters. In India, strings are commonly used to represent names, addresses, and greetings.

```python
greeting = "Namaste, Bharat!"
print(greeting, type(greeting))  # Output: Namaste, Bharat! <class 'str'>
```

Strings can be enclosed in single quotes (') or double quotes ("), both of which are widely used in Indian languages for words like "सुप्रभात" (Good Morning).

c) Boolean Data Type

i. Boolean (bool): Represents truth values. In everyday Indian life, booleans can be used to determine conditions like whether a person has paid for a train ticket or not.

```
ticket_paid = True
print(ticket_paid, type(ticket_paid))  # Output: True <class 'bool'>
```

Booleans have two values: True and False.

d) Container Data Types

Python also provides container types, which are used to store collections of data. These are the building blocks for more complex data structures.

i. List (list): An ordered collection of items, which can be modified. Lists are very useful in Python when managing collections of data like a list of Indian festivals or shopping items.

```
indian_festivals = ["Diwali", "Holi", "Dussehra", "Navratri"]
print(indian_festivals, type(indian_festivals))  # Output: ['Diwali', 'Holi', 'Dussehra', 'Navratri'] <class 'list'>
```

ii. Tuple (tuple): An ordered collection of items, but unlike lists, tuples are immutable (cannot be modified). You can use tuples to represent unchangeable data, like coordinates of a famous temple in India.

```
temple_coordinates = (19.0760, 72.8777)  # Coordinates of a temple in Mumbai
print(temple_coordinates, type(temple_coordinates))  # Output: (19.0760, 72.8777) <class 'tuple'>
```

iii. Dictionary (dict): A collection of key-value pairs, useful for representing data like student marks or address details.

```
student_marks = {
    "Aarav": 85,
    "Madhavi": 90,
    "Rohan": 75
}
print(student_marks, type(student_marks))  # Output: {'Aarav': 85, 'Madhavi': 90, 'Rohan': 75} <class 'dict'>
```

iv. Set (set): A collection of unique items that are unordered. Sets are commonly used in scenarios like tracking unique Indian spices in a kitchen.

```
spices = {"turmeric", "cumin", "cloves", "cardamom"}
print(spices, type(spices))  # Output: {'turmeric', 'cumin', 'cloves', 'cardamom'} <class 'set'>
```

e) Type Conversion (Casting)

Python allows us to convert one data type to another, a process known as type casting. This is useful when working with data that needs to be transformed into different forms, like converting a string representing a price into a numeric value.

int(): Converts a value to an integer.

float(): Converts a value to a floating-point number.

str(): Converts a value to a string.

Example of converting a string to an integer:

string_value = "100"

int_value = int(string_value)

print(int_value, type(int_value)) # Output: 100 <class 'int'>

2.2 Tokens in Python

In Python, tokens are the smallest units of code that hold meaning, just like words and sentences in a language. These tokens can be categorized into various types.

a) Keywords

Keywords are reserved words that Python uses for its syntax and control flow. They cannot be used as variable names or identifiers. In Indian culture, think of keywords as mantras—predefined words that have special meaning in the language.

Examples of Python keywords:

if, else, for, while, def, class, return, break

b) Identifiers

Identifiers are names used to identify variables, functions, classes, and other objects in Python. In India, identifiers can be thought of as names of individuals or places—unique and significant.

Examples of valid identifiers:

student_age, temple_location, mango_count

c) Literals

Literals represent constant values used in Python, like the numbers or text you work with daily. In India, these could be the cost of an item or a name of a festival.

123 # Integer literal

"Diwali" # String literal

3.14 # Float literal

d) Operators

Operators in Python perform various operations on variables and values. Think of them as the "actions" in your program. Operators can be compared to various tools used in traditional occupations like farming or cooking.

Types of operators in Python:

i.   Arithmetic Operators: Used to perform mathematical operations.

addition = 2 + 3 # 5

subtraction = 7 - 3 # 4

multiplication = 4 * 5 # 20

ii.   Relational Operators: Used to compare values.

5 == 5 # True

5 > 3 # True

iii.   Logical Operators: Used to combine multiple conditions.

True and False # False

e) Delimiters

Delimiters in Python help in separating elements in a program. They are like punctuation marks in an Indian story that help structure sentences.

Example:

Parentheses (): Used for function calls and grouping expressions.

Brackets []: Used for lists and indexing.

Braces {}: Used for dictionaries and sets.

2.3 Operator Precedence and Associativity

Operator precedence determines the order in which operators are evaluated in an expression. In India, this can be compared to the prioritization of tasks during a festival—some activities must be done before others.

a) Precedence

Python evaluates operators with higher precedence before those with lower precedence. For example, multiplication has a higher precedence than addition.

Example:

result = 3 + 5 * 2 # Output: 13 (Multiplication first)

b) Associativity

If operators have the same precedence, their associativity determines the order of evaluation. Most operators in Python are left-associative, meaning they are evaluated from left to right.

Example:

result = 10 - 5 + 2 # Output: 7 (Evaluated as (10 - 5) + 2)

Exponentiation (**) is a right-associative operator:

result = 2 ** 3 ** 2 # Output: 512 (Evaluated as 2 ** (3 ** 2))

2.4 Python Input and Output Functions

Python provides built-in functions for interacting with the user and displaying output.

a) Input Function

The input() function is used to get input from the user. In India, think of this as asking for someone's name at a traditional wedding.

Example:

name = input("Enter your name: ")

print(f"Namaste, {name}!") # Output: Namaste, Aarav!

b) Output Function

The print() function is used to output data to the console. It's like announcing the winner of a traditional Indian game.

Example:

print("Welcome to the Python world!")

You can also format output using f-strings, which is a simple and powerful way to include variables in your printed messages.

Example:

age = 25

print(f"Your age is {age}") # Output: Your age is 25

2.5 Python Escape Sequence Characters

Escape sequences in Python allow you to insert special characters into strings, like new lines or tabs, which is similar to creating space between lines of poetry or songs in Indian culture.

Example:

Newline (\n): Moves text to a new line.

```
print("Hello\nWorld")

# Output:

# Hello

# World
```

Tab (\t): Adds a tab space.

```
print("Name\tAge")

print("Aarav\t25")

# Output:

# Name   Age

# Aarav  25
```

2.6 Type and ID Functions

The type() function in Python is used to determine the type of an object, similar to identifying the variety of mangoes during the season. The id() function returns a unique identifier for each object, akin to a fingerprint.

Example:

```
name = "Rani"

print(type(name))  # Output: <class 'str'>

print(id(name))    # Output: Unique ID for the string object
```

In this chapter, we've explored the foundational concepts of Python, using real-life examples that tie into the cultural and practical aspects of India. By understanding these basic concepts, you're well on your way to becoming proficient in Python programming.

2.7 Exercise Questions

1. Working with Data Types

a) Write a Python program to store the names of three Indian cities in a list and print their names.
b) Create a program that stores the price of turmeric per kilogram (in float) and the number of kilograms bought (integer). Calculate and print the total cost.

2. Numeric Operations

a) Write a program to calculate the total amount spent on 3 items: ₹50, ₹75.50, and ₹120.75.
b) Define a complex number z = 4 + 3j. Print its real and imaginary parts separately.

3. String Manipulation

a) Write a program to take an input string, "Namaste," and append "Bharat" to it using concatenation. Print the result.
b) Extract and print the first 4 characters of the string "IncredibleIndia".

4. Boolean Logic

a) Write a Python program that checks if a given number is greater than 10 and less than 50. Print True or False accordingly.
b) Implement a program that checks if a number is divisible by both 5 and 7.

5. Type Conversion

a) Write a program to convert the string "500" to an integer and multiply it by 2.
b) Convert the float 150.25 into a string and print its type.

6. Input and Output

a) Write a Python program to take the name and age of a user as input and print a greeting message like, "Namaste, [Name]! You are [Age] years old."
b) Take two numbers as input and display their sum using formatted output.

7. Identifying Errors in Code

a) Find the error in the following code snippet and correct it:

```
name = "Aarav"

print("Hello, name")
```

b) Identify the error in the following code and provide the correct version:

```
num = 25.5

result = num // 3

print("The result is: " + result)
```

8. Logical Operators

a) Write a Python program to check if a number is positive and even using logical operators.
b) Create a program that checks if a given number is divisible by 3 or 7 but not both.

9. Membership Operators

a) Write a program to check if "Holi" is present in the list ["Diwali", "Holi", "Dussehra"].
b) Use not in to check if "Christmas" is not present in the same list.

10. Identity Operators

a) Write a program to demonstrate the use of is by comparing two variables pointing to the same integer.
b) Use is not to compare two lists with identical elements but different memory addresses.

11. Operator Precedence

a) Evaluate the expression 5 + 3 * 2 ** 2 using operator precedence and print the result.

b) Write a program to compute (10 + 5) * 2 ** 2 and print the result.

12. Escape Sequences

a) Write a Python program to print the following using escape sequences:

Welcome to Python!

Let's learn and grow together.

b) Write a program to display the tabular format:

```
Name    Age
Aarav   21
Meera   19
```

13. Functions: type() and id()

a) Write a program that creates a variable price = 100.50 and prints its type and ID.

b) Demonstrate that two variables referring to the same string have the same ID.

14. Error Debugging

a) Find and fix the issue in the code below:

```
festival_list = ["Diwali", "Holi", "Dussehra"]
print(festival_list[3])
b) Debug the following code:
amount = 1000
print("The total amount is: " + amount)
```

15. Working with Delimiters

a) Create a Python dictionary to store train timings using {}. Print the value of a specific key.

b) Use square brackets to create a list of your favorite Indian dishes and print the second item.

16. Practical Applications

a) Write a Python program to calculate the cost of 5 items, each priced differently. Use input to take the prices.

b) Create a program to store the number of students in different Indian states and print the total number of students.

17. Real-life Scenarios

a) Write a Python program that takes the number of mangoes harvested in three Indian states and calculates the average harvest.

b) Create a program to display a personalized greeting based on the time of day (e.g., "Good Morning," "Good Evening"). Use input() to take the user's name and current time. [**Note:** Decision making systems will be discussed in the upcoming chapter.]

Solutions

1. Working with Data Types

a)

```python
cities = ["Delhi", "Mumbai", "Kolkata"]
for city in cities:
    print(city)
```

b)

```python
price_per_kg = 250.5
quantity = 3
total_cost = price_per_kg * quantity
print("Total cost of turmeric: ₹", total_cost)
```

2. Numeric Operations

a)

```python
item1 = 50
item2 = 75.50
item3 = 120.75
total = item1 + item2 + item3
print("Total amount spent: ₹", total)
```

b)

```python
z = 4 + 3j
print("Real part:", z.real)
print("Imaginary part:", z.imag)
```

3. String Manipulation

a)

```python
greeting = "Namaste"
full_greeting = greeting + " Bharat"
print(full_greeting)
```

b)

```python
string = "IncredibleIndia"
print("First 4 characters:", string[:4])
```

4. Boolean Logic

a)

```python
number = 25
result = number > 10 and number < 50
print(result)
```

b)

```python
number = 35
result = number % 5 == 0 and number % 7 == 0
print(result)
```

5. Type Conversion

a)

```python
value = "500"
converted_value = int(value) * 2
print(converted_value)
```

b)

```python
float_value = 150.25
string_value = str(float_value)
print("Type:", type(string_value))
```

6. Input and Output

a)

```python
name = input("Enter your name: ")
age = input("Enter your age: ")
print(f"Namaste, {name}! You are {age} years old.")
```

b)

```python
num1 = int(input("Enter the first number: "))
num2 = int(input("Enter the second number: "))
```

```python
print(f"The sum of {num1} and {num2} is {num1 + num2}")
```

7. Identifying Errors in Code

a)

```python
name = "Aarav"
print(f"Hello, {name}")  # Corrected: Used f-string for dynamic variable reference
```

b)

```python
num = 25.5
result = num // 3
print("The result is:", result)  # Corrected: Added `,` to concatenate string and variable
```

8. Logical Operators

a)

```python
number = 8
print(number > 0 and number % 2 == 0)
```

b)

```python
number = 21
print((number % 3 == 0 or number % 7 == 0) and not (number % 3 == 0 and number % 7 == 0))
```

9. Membership Operators

a)

```python
festivals = ["Diwali", "Holi", "Dussehra"]
print("Holi" in festivals)
```

b)

```python
print("Christmas" not in festivals)
```

10. Identity Operators

a)

```python
x = 100
y = 100
print(x is y)  # True because integers with same value share memory
```

b)

```python
list1 = [1, 2, 3]

list2 = [1, 2, 3]

print(list1 is not list2)  # True because lists have different memory locations
```

11. Operator Precedence

a)

```python
result = 5 + 3 * 2 ** 2

print(result)  # Output: 17
```

b)

```python
result = (10 + 5) * 2 ** 2

print(result)  # Output: 60
```

12. Escape Sequences

a)

```python
print("Welcome to Python!\nLet's learn and grow together.")
```

b)

```python
print("Name\tAge\nAarav\t21\nMeera\t19")
```

13. Functions: type() and id()

a)

```python
price = 100.50

print("Type:", type(price))

print("ID:", id(price))
```

b)

```python
string1 = "Python"

string2 = "Python"

print(id(string1) == id(string2))  # True because strings with same content share memory
```

14. Error Debugging

a)

```python
festival_list = ["Diwali", "Holi", "Dussehra"]

print(festival_list[2])  # Fixed: Corrected the index from 3 to 2
```

b)

```python
amount = 1000

print("The total amount is:", amount)  # Fixed: Used `,` instead of `+` for concatenation
```

15. Working with Delimiters

a)

```python
train_timings = {"Delhi-Mumbai": "10:00 AM", "Mumbai-Chennai": "5:00 PM"}

print(train_timings["Delhi-Mumbai"])
```

b)

```python
dishes = ["Biryani", "Dosa", "Paneer Tikka"]

print(dishes[1])
```

16. Practical Applications

a)

```python
item1 = float(input("Enter the price of item 1: "))

item2 = float(input("Enter the price of item 2: "))

item3 = float(input("Enter the price of item 3: "))

item4 = float(input("Enter the price of item 4: "))

item5 = float(input("Enter the price of item 5: "))

total_cost = item1 + item2 + item3 + item4 + item5

print("Total cost:", total_cost)
```

b)

```python
students = {"Karnataka": 500, "Tamil Nadu": 600, "Kerala": 400}

total_students = sum(students.values())

print("Total number of students:", total_students)
```

17. Real-life Scenarios

a)

```python
state1 = int(input("Enter the number of mangoes harvested in state 1: "))

state2 = int(input("Enter the number of mangoes harvested in state 2: "))

state3 = int(input("Enter the number of mangoes harvested in state 3: "))
```

```python
average = (state1 + state2 + state3) / 3

print("Average harvest:", average)
```

b)

```python
name = input("Enter your name: ")

current_time = int(input("Enter the current hour (0-23): "))

if current_time < 12:

    greeting = "Good Morning"

elif current_time < 18:

    greeting = "Good Afternoon"

else:

    greeting = "Good Evening"

print(f"{greeting}, {name}!")
```

2.8 Check Your Logic

1. **Numeric Data Types**:
   Write a Python program to calculate the average of three test scores: 88, 92, and 75.

2. **String Operations**:
   Create a program to concatenate two strings: "Incredible" and "India", and print the resulting string.

3. **Escape Sequences**:
   Write a program to display the following text using escape sequences:

Hello, Python!

   - Let's learn

   - And explore

4. **Input and Type Conversion**:
   Write a program that takes the price of a meal (as a string) and converts it to a float. Then calculate a 10% tip and print the total amount to be paid.

5. **Operator Precedence**:
   Write a Python program to compute the result of 20 + 10 / 2 ** 2 - 5 step by step.

6. **Arithmetic Operations**:
   Write a program to calculate the area of a rectangle with a length of 12.5 meters and a breadth of 7.8 meters.

7. **Bitwise Operations**:
   Perform a bitwise AND and OR operation on the numbers 6 and 3. Display the results.

8. **Membership Operators**:
   Write a Python program to check if the letter 'a' is present in the string "Namaste".

9. **Type Function**:
   Create a program that takes an input from the user and prints its data type using the type() function.

10. **ID Function**:
    Write a Python program to demonstrate that two variables holding the same integer value share the same memory address using the id() function.

Solutions

1. Numeric Data Types

```
score1 = 88

score2 = 92

score3 = 75

average = (score1 + score2 + score3) / 3

print("The average score is:", average)
```

2. String Operations

```
string1 = "Incredible"

string2 = "India"

result = string1 + string2

print("Concatenated string:", result)
```

3. Escape Sequences

```
print("Hello, Python!\n\t- Let's learn\n\t- And explore")
```

4. Input and Type Conversion

```
meal_price = input("Enter the price of the meal: ")

meal_price = float(meal_price)

tip = meal_price * 0.10

total_amount = meal_price + tip

print("The total amount to be paid is:", total_amount)
```

5. Operator Precedence

```
result = 20 + 10 / 2 ** 2 - 5
```

```python
# Step-by-step:

# 2 ** 2 = 4

# 10 / 4 = 2.5

# 20 + 2.5 = 22.5

# 22.5 - 5 = 17.5

print("The result is:", result)
```

6. Arithmetic Operations

```python
length = 12.5

breadth = 7.8

area = length * breadth

print("The area of the rectangle is:", area, "square meters")
```

7. Bitwise Operations

```python
a = 6  # Binary: 110

b = 3  # Binary: 011

bitwise_and = a & b  # Binary: 010 -> Decimal: 2

bitwise_or = a | b   # Binary: 111 -> Decimal: 7

print("Bitwise AND:", bitwise_and)

print("Bitwise OR:", bitwise_or)
```

8. Membership Operators

```python
word = "Namaste"
if 'a' in word:
    print("The letter 'a' is present in the word.")
else:
    print("The letter 'a' is not present in the word.")
```

9. Type Function

```python
user_input = input("Enter something: ")

print("The data type of the input is:", type(user_input))
```

10. ID Function

x = 42

y = 42

print("ID of x:", id(x))

print("ID of y:", id(y))

print("Do x and y share the same memory location?", id(x) == id(y))

Scenario-Based Question 1: "A Day in the Life of a Python Programmer"

Scenario

Arjun, a new Python programmer, is automating a small-scale food delivery service in India. The service offers three meals per day: breakfast, lunch, and dinner. Arjun's task is to write a Python program to calculate daily earnings and provide a detailed report.

Requirements

1. **Data Initialization**:
   Store the meal prices in appropriate variables:

   - Breakfast: ₹50
   - Lunch: ₹120
   - Dinner: ₹150

2. **User Input**:
   Ask the user how many breakfasts, lunches, and dinners were sold. Use the appropriate data type to store this information.

3. **Perform Calculations**:
   a) Calculate the total earnings for each meal type.
   b) Compute the total earnings for the day by summing up the meal-specific totals.

4. **Output**:
   Display the following detailed report using formatted strings:

Food Delivery Report:

Breakfast: ₹<breakfast_total>

Lunch: ₹<lunch_total>

Dinner: ₹<dinner_total>

Total Earnings: ₹<total_earnings>

5. **Operator Precedence**:
   In the calculations, ensure you apply the correct precedence for multiplication and addition.

6. Save it as food_delivery.py and execute it as a standalone script.

Solution

Here's the program Arjun might write:

```python
# Food Delivery Automation Script

# Initialize meal prices

breakfast_price = 50

lunch_price = 120

dinner_price = 150


# Input: Number of meals sold

num_breakfast = int(input("Enter the number of breakfasts sold: "))

num_lunch = int(input("Enter the number of lunches sold: "))

num_dinner = int(input("Enter the number of dinners sold: "))


# Calculations: Total earnings for each meal and overall

breakfast_earnings = num_breakfast * breakfast_price

lunch_earnings = num_lunch * lunch_price

dinner_earnings = num_dinner * dinner_price

total_earnings = breakfast_earnings + lunch_earnings + dinner_earnings


# Output: Detailed report

print("\nFood Delivery Report:")

print("--------------------")

print(f"Breakfast: ₹{breakfast_earnings}")

print(f"Lunch: ₹{lunch_earnings}")

print(f"Dinner: ₹{dinner_earnings}")
```

```python
print("--------------------")
```

```python
print(f"Total Earnings: ₹{total_earnings}")
```

Scenario-Based Question 2: "Track Your Expenses with Python"

Scenario

Maya is managing her monthly expenses and wants to use Python to automate her calculations. Her expenses include rent, groceries, utilities, and entertainment. She needs a Python program to help:

1. **Initialize the expense categories and their respective amounts.**

2. **Calculate the total monthly expenses.**

3. **Determine how much of her ₹50,000 monthly income remains after expenses.**

4. **Display a formatted summary of her expenses.**

Task

Maya has asked you to write a Python program that performs the following:

1. **Initialize Data**: Store the amounts spent on the following categories as variables:

   - Rent: ₹20,000
   - Groceries: ₹8,000
   - Utilities: ₹5,000
   - Entertainment: ₹3,000

2. **Perform Calculations**:
   a) Calculate the total expenses for the month.
   b) Compute the remaining balance from her ₹50,000 monthly income.

3. **Output**:
   Provide a detailed summary in the following format:

Expense Report:

Rent: ₹<rent_amount>

Groceries: ₹<groceries_amount>

Utilities: ₹<utilities_amount>

Entertainment: ₹<entertainment_amount>

Total Expenses: ₹<total_expenses>

Remaining Balance: ₹<remaining_balance>

4. **Scripting Mode**: Save the program as expense_tracker.py and execute it.

Solution

```python
# Expense Tracker Script

# Step 1: Initialize expense data

rent = 20000

groceries = 8000

utilities = 5000

entertainment = 3000

# Step 2: Perform calculations

total_expenses = rent + groceries + utilities + entertainment

monthly_income = 50000

remaining_balance = monthly_income - total_expenses


# Step 3: Output the expense report

print("\nExpense Report:")

print("--------------------")

print(f"Rent: ₹{rent}")

print(f"Groceries: ₹{groceries}")

print(f"Utilities: ₹{utilities}")

print(f"Entertainment: ₹{entertainment}")

print("--------------------")

print(f"Total Expenses: ₹{total_expenses}")

print(f"Remaining Balance: ₹{remaining_balance}")
```

3. Python Conditional Statements

In this chapter, we will learn about **conditional statements** in Python. Conditional statements allow a program to execute different blocks of code based on certain conditions, making it possible to control the flow of execution. Understanding conditional statements is crucial for decision-making in programming, where different actions are performed depending on whether a condition is true or false.

3.1 Introduction to Conditional Statements

Conditional statements in Python are used to make decisions within a program. When certain conditions are met, specific code is executed; otherwise, it is skipped. These statements are essential for making your program respond to different situations and inputs.

For example, you might want your program to print "Good Morning" if the time is before noon, and "Good Evening" if it is after noon. This can be achieved using conditional statements.

3.2 Types of Decision-Making Statements

There are several types of decision-making statements in Python:

1. **if statement**

2. **if-else statement**

3. **if-elif-else statement**

4. **nested if statement**

5. **match statement** (introduced in Python 3.10)

Each type allows you to check conditions in different ways.

3.3 The if Statement

The if statement is the simplest form of decision-making in Python. It allows you to check a condition and run a block of code if the condition is true.

Syntax:

```
if condition:
    # code block to execute if the condition is true
```

Example:

```
x = 10
if x > 5:
    print("x is greater than 5")
```

Explanation:

The condition x > 5 is evaluated. Since x is 10, which is greater than 5, the block of code inside the if statement will be executed, and the output will be:

x is greater than 5

If the condition is false, the block of code inside the if statement is skipped.

3.4 The if-else Statement

The if-else statement extends the if statement by allowing you to execute one block of code if the condition is true and another block if the condition is false.

Syntax:

```
if condition:
    # code block to execute if the condition is true
else:
    # code block to execute if the condition is false
```

Example:

```
x = 2
if x > 3:
    print("x is greater than 3")
else:
    print("x is not greater than 3")
```

Explanation:

The condition x > 3 is false because x is 2. Therefore, the program will execute the code inside the else block and print:

x is not greater than 3

3.5 The if-elif-else Statement

The if-elif-else statement allows you to check multiple conditions in sequence. The first condition that evaluates to true will execute its corresponding block of code, and the rest of the conditions will be skipped.

Syntax:

```
if condition1:
    # code block to execute if condition1 is true
elif condition2:
    # code block to execute if condition2 is true
```

```
else:
    # code block to execute if all conditions are false
```

Example:

```
x = 10
if x < 10:
    print("x is less than 10")
elif x == 10:
    print("x is equal to 10")
else:
    print("x is greater than 10")
```

Explanation:

The condition x == 10 is true because x is 10. Therefore, the program will execute the code under the elif block and print:

```
x is equal to 10
```

If none of the if or elif conditions are true, the code inside the else block will be executed.

3.6 Nested if Statements

Nested if statements allow you to check conditions within another condition. This can be useful when you need to check multiple levels of conditions.

Syntax:

```
if condition1:
    if condition2:
        # code block if both conditions are true
    else:
        # code block if condition2 is false
else:
    # code block if condition1 is false
```

Example:

```
x = 10
y = 5
if x > 5:
    if y > 3:
```

```python
    print("x is greater than 5 and y is greater than 3")

  else:

    print("x is greater than 5 but y is not greater than 3")

else:

  print("x is not greater than 5")
```

Explanation:

First, the program checks if x > 5. Since x is 10, this condition is true. Then, the program checks if y > 3. Since y is 5, which is greater than 3, the output will be:

x is greater than 5 and y is greater than 3

3.7 The match Statement (Python 3.10+)

The match statement, introduced in Python 3.10, provides a more elegant way to match patterns against values. It is similar to the switch statement in other programming languages and is used for matching multiple conditions in a more readable manner.

Syntax:

```python
match expression:

  case pattern1:

    # code block for pattern1

  case pattern2:

    # code block for pattern2

  case _:

    # default case if no patterns match
```

Example:

```python
def describe_number(num):

  match num:

    case 0:

      print("Zero")

    case 1:

      print("One")

    case 2:

      print("Two")

    case _:
```

    print("Other")

describe_number(1)

Explanation:

The function checks the value of num and matches it with different cases. Since num is 1, the corresponding code block will be executed and print:

One

The _ case acts as a "catch-all" and is executed if no other case matches.

3.8 Indentation in Python

Indentation in Python is not just for readability; it determines the structure of the code. Unlike many other languages, Python does not use braces {} to mark code blocks. Instead, it uses indentation to signify which statements belong to which block.

Importance of Indentation:

- Indentation is required to define the scope of statements within if, else, loops, functions, and classes.

- Python requires that all lines in a block must be indented the same amount.

- Typically, 4 spaces are used for each level of indentation.

Example:

x = 10

if x > 5:

    print("x is greater than 5")

    if x > 7:

        print("x is also greater than 7")

In this example, the second print statement is nested under the first if block, indicating it is part of the nested condition.

3.9 Best Practices for Conditional Statements and Indentation

1. **Use Consistent Indentation**:

    Always use the same number of spaces (typically 4) for each level of indentation. Avoid mixing spaces and tabs.

2. **Clarity in Conditions**:
    Write clear and simple conditions. Use logical operators like and, or, and not to create more complex conditions when necessary.

3. **Keep the Code Readable**:
    Always keep your conditional statements clean and easy to understand. Avoid nesting too deeply, as it may make the code hard to follow.

By the end of this chapter, you should be comfortable with writing conditional statements in Python to handle a variety of situations in your programs. Conditional logic is a core concept in programming, and mastering it is crucial for writing efficient and dynamic code. Now let's learn the concepts of this unit with examples.

3.10 Exercise Questions

1. **Simple if Statement**

    Write a Python program that checks if a given number is positive. If it is, print "Positive Number".

2. **if-else Statement**

    Write a Python program that checks if a number is even or odd and prints the result.

3. **Multiple if Statements**

    Write a Python program that checks whether a given number is greater than 100, less than 50, or between 50 and 100. Print a suitable message for each case.

4. **if-elif-else Statement**

    Write a Python program that takes an integer input from the user and checks whether the number is negative, zero, or positive.

5. **Nested if Statement**

    Write a Python program to check if a number is divisible by both 5 and 7. If it is, print "Divisible by both 5 and 7". Otherwise, print "Not divisible by both".

6. **match Statement (Pattern Matching)**

    Write a Python program that uses a match statement to check if a given number is 1, 2, or 3. Print a suitable message for each case.

7. **Using if-else for Voting Eligibility**

    Write a Python program that takes a person's age as input and checks if the person is eligible to vote (18 or older). Print the appropriate message.

8. **if with Logical Operators**

    Write a Python program that checks if a given number is both greater than 10 and divisible by 3. Print "True" if both conditions are met, otherwise print "False".

9. **Checking Multiple Conditions**

    Write a Python program to check if a number is both divisible by 5 and not divisible by 7. Print a suitable message based on the result.

10. **Correcting the Code (Error Identification)**

Identify the error in the following code and correct it:

```
x = 15
if x > 10
    print("x is greater than 10")
```

11. **Correcting the Code (Error Identification)**

Find and fix the error in the following code:

```
x = 10
if x = 10:
    print("x is 10")
```

12. **Nested if Statements**

Write a Python program that checks if a number is greater than 10, and if true, checks if it is also divisible by 3. Print an appropriate message based on both conditions.

13. **Using elif for Range Check**

Write a Python program that checks if a number is between 1 and 100 (inclusive). If it is, print "In range", otherwise print "Out of range".

14. **if Statement with String Input**

Write a Python program that takes a string input and checks if it is "Python". If it is, print "Correct", otherwise print "Incorrect".

15. **Correcting the Code (Error Identification)**

Fix the error in the following code snippet:

```
x = 12
if x > 10:
    print("x is greater than 10")
else:
    print("x is less than or equal to 10")
```

16. **match Statement with List**

Write a Python program that uses a match statement to check if a list is empty, has one element, or has multiple elements. Print a message based on the result.

17. **Checking Even and Odd Numbers**

Write a Python program that checks if a number is even or odd using an if-else statement. If even, print "Even", else print "Odd".

18. **Using if-else for Temperature**

Write a Python program that takes the temperature as input and checks if it's below 0 (cold), between 0 and 20 (cool), or above 20 (warm). Print the appropriate message for each case.

19. **Correcting the Code (Error Identification)**

Find the error in the following code and correct it:

```python
num1 = 10
num2 = 20
if num1 > num2:
    print("num1 is greater")
elif num1 < num2
    print("num2 is greater")
```

20. **if-else for Largest Number**

Write a Python program to find the largest of three numbers using if-else statements.

Solutions

1. Simple if Statement

```python
number = int(input("Enter a number: "))
if number > 0:
    print("Positive Number")
```

2. if-else Statement

```python
number = int(input("Enter a number: "))
if number % 2 == 0:
    print("Even")
else:
    print("Odd")
```

3. Multiple if Statements

```python
number = int(input("Enter a number: "))
if number > 100:
    print("Greater than 100")
elif number < 50:
    print("Less than 50")
else:
```

```python
print("Between 50 and 100")
```

4. if-elif-else Statement

```python
number = int(input("Enter a number: "))
if number < 0:
    print("Negative")
elif number == 0:
    print("Zero")
else:
    print("Positive")
```

5. Nested if Statement

```python
number = int(input("Enter a number: "))
if number % 5 == 0:
    if number % 7 == 0:
        print("Divisible by both 5 and 7")
    else:
        print("Divisible by 5 but not 7")
else:
    print("Not divisible by 5")
```

6. match Statement (Pattern Matching)

```python
number = int(input("Enter a number (1, 2, or 3): "))
match number:
    case 1:
        print("One")
    case 2:
        print("Two")
    case 3:
        print("Three")
    case _:
        print("Other")
```

7. Using if-else for Voting Eligibility

```python
age = int(input("Enter your age: "))

if age >= 18:

    print("You are eligible to vote.")

else:

    print("You are not eligible to vote.")
```

8. if with Logical Operators

```python
number = int(input("Enter a number: "))

if number > 10 and number % 3 == 0:

    print("True")

else:

    print("False")
```

9. Checking Multiple Conditions

```python
number = int(input("Enter a number: "))

if number % 5 == 0 and number % 7 != 0:

    print("Divisible by 5 but not by 7")

else:

    print("Does not satisfy the condition")
```

10. Correcting the Code (Error Identification)

```python
x = 15

if x > 10:

    print("x is greater than 10")
```

11. Correcting the Code (Error Identification)

```python
x = 10

if x == 10:

    print("x is 10")
```

12. Nested if Statements

```python
number = int(input("Enter a number: "))

if number > 10:

    if number % 3 == 0:

        print("Greater than 10 and divisible by 3")
```

```python
else:
    print("Greater than 10 but not divisible by 3")
else:
print("Not greater than 10")
```

13. Using elif for Range Check

```python
number = int(input("Enter a number: "))
if 1 <= number <= 100:
    print("In range")
else:
    print("Out of range")
```

14. if Statement with String Input

```python
string = input("Enter a string: ")
if string == "Python":
    print("Correct")
else:
    print("Incorrect")
```

15. Correcting the Code (Error Identification)

```python
x = 12
if x > 10:
    print("x is greater than 10")
else:
    print("x is less than or equal to 10")
```

16. match Statement with List

```python
data = [1, 2, 3]
match data:
    case []:
        print("Empty list")
    case [first, *rest]:
        print(f"First element: {first}, Rest: {rest}")
    case _:
```

```python
    print("Other data structure")
```

17. Checking Even and Odd Numbers

```python
number = int(input("Enter a number: "))
if number % 2 == 0:
    print("Even")
else:
    print("Odd")
```

18. Using if-else for Temperature

```python
temp = int(input("Enter temperature: "))
if temp < 0:
    print("Cold")
elif 0 <= temp <= 20:
    print("Cool")
else:
    print("Warm")
```

19. Correcting the Code (Error Identification)

```python
num1 = 10
num2 = 20
if num1 > num2:
    print("num1 is greater")
elif num1 < num2:
    print("num2 is greater")
```

20. if-else for Largest Number

```python
a = 10
b = 20
c = 30
if a > b and a > c:
    print("a is the largest")
elif b > a and b > c:
    print("b is the largest")
```

```
else:

    print("c is the largest")
```

3.11 Check your Logic: Scenario-Based Questions

Scenario 1: Checking Discount Eligibility

Scenario:
Ravi runs a small online clothing store in India. He wants to offer a discount to customers who make purchases above a certain amount. The discount is as follows:

- 10% for purchases above ₹1,000 but less than ₹5,000.

- 20% for purchases above ₹5,000.

Write a Python program that:

1. Takes the total amount of the customer's purchase as input.

2. Checks if the customer is eligible for a discount based on the purchase amount.

3. Calculates and prints the final price after applying the discount.

4. If the purchase amount is less than ₹1,000, print "No discount available."

Scenario 2: Checking a Student's Grades

Scenario:
Shreya is a teacher at a school and needs a program to determine the grade of her students based on their marks. The grading system is as follows:

- Marks 90 and above: Grade A

- Marks between 80 and 89: Grade B

- Marks between 70 and 79: Grade C

- Marks below 70: Grade D

Write a Python program that:

1. Takes the student's marks as input.

2. Determines the grade based on the marks and prints the corresponding grade.

3. If the marks are below 70, print "Below average performance."

Scenario 3: Movie Ticket Pricing

Scenario:

Ajay is managing a movie theater, and he offers different ticket prices based on the customer's age group:

- Adults (18 years and older): ₹300 per ticket.

- Students (between 12 and 17 years): ₹150 per ticket.

- Children (below 12 years): Free ticket.

Write a Python program that:

1. Takes the customer's age as input.

2. Determines the ticket price based on the age group.

3. Prints the corresponding ticket price or "Free" if the customer is a child.

4. If the customer is younger than 0 or older than 100, print "Invalid age."

Solution

1. **Solution: Checking Discount Eligibility**

```python
# Input: Total purchase amount

purchase_amount = float(input("Enter the total amount of your purchase: ₹"))


# Checking eligibility for discount

if purchase_amount >= 1000 and purchase_amount < 5000:

    discount = 0.10  # 10% discount

    final_price = purchase_amount - (purchase_amount * discount)

    print(f"You are eligible for a 10% discount. Final price after discount: ₹{final_price}")

elif purchase_amount >= 5000:

    discount = 0.20  # 20% discount

    final_price = purchase_amount - (purchase_amount * discount)

    print(f"You are eligible for a 20% discount. Final price after discount: ₹{final_price}")

else:

    print("No discount available.")
```

2. Solution: Checking a Student's Grades

```python
# Input: Student's marks

marks = float(input("Enter the student's marks: "))
```

```python
# Determine the grade
if marks >= 90:
    print("Grade A")
elif 80 <= marks < 90:
    print("Grade B")
elif 70 <= marks < 80:
    print("Grade C")
else:
    print("Below average performance")
```

3. Solution: Movie Ticket Pricing

```python
# Input: Customer's age
age = int(input("Enter your age: "))
# Determine the ticket price based on age
if age >= 18:
    print("Ticket price: ₹300 (Adult)")
elif 12 <= age < 18:
    print("Ticket price: ₹150 (Student)")
elif age < 12 and age >= 0:
    print("Ticket price: Free (Child)")
else:
    print("Invalid age.")
```

4. Loops In Python

Loops are one of the core programming concepts that allow you to execute a block of code multiple times. They are essential for tasks such as iterating over a sequence, automating repetitive operations, or performing an action until a specific condition is met. Python offers a few different types of loops: the **for loop**, the **while loop**, and **nested loops**, among others. In this chapter, we will cover how these loops work in Python, along with their syntax, usage, and examples.

4.1 Introduction to Loops in Python

Loops in Python enable the repeated execution of a block of code as long as a specified condition is true. Loops are used in a variety of applications, such as iterating through a collection, automating repetitive tasks, and performing tasks multiple times with slight variations.

Key Points:

- **For Loop**: Used to iterate over a sequence like a list, string, or range.

- **While Loop**: Used to repeat a block of code as long as a given condition remains true.

- **Nested Loops**: A loop inside another loop, useful for working with multi-dimensional data.

Example 1: Simple for loop

```python
for i in range(3):
    print(f"Iteration {i}")
```

Explanation: This loop will print the iteration count from 0 to 2.

Example 2: Simple while loop

```python
count = 0
while count < 3:
    print(f"Count: {count}")
    count += 1
```

Explanation: This while loop will also print the count from 0 to 2.

4.2 Types of Loops in Python

Python supports two main types of loops:

1. **For Loop**

2. **While Loop**

Each type of loop has specific use cases, strengths, and weaknesses.

4.3 The For Loop

The for loop in Python is used to iterate over a sequence (such as a list, string, or range) and execute a block of code for each item in the sequence. It's the most commonly used loop in Python for iterating over collections.

Syntax:

```
for item in sequence:
    # code block to execute
```

Example 1: Iterating over a list of fruits

```
fruits = ["apple", "banana", "cherry"]
for fruit in fruits:
    print(fruit)
```

Output:

```
banana
cherry
```

Explanation: This loop iterates over each element in the list fruits and prints it.

Example 2: Using a for loop with range()

```
for i in range(5):
    print(i)
```

Output:

```
0
1
2
3
4
```

Explanation: The range(5) generates a sequence of numbers from 0 to 4, and the loop iterates over them.

4.4 The While Loop

The while loop in Python runs as long as the given condition is true. It's useful when you don't know in advance how many iterations you need to make, but you do have a condition to evaluate.

Syntax:

```
while condition:
    # code block to execute
```

Example 1: Counting with a while loop

```
count = 0
```

```
while count < 3:

    print(f"Count: {count}")

    count += 1
```

Output:

Count: 0

Count: 1

Count: 2

Explanation: The loop continues as long as count is less than 3, printing the count on each iteration.

Example 2: Infinite loop (with a break)

```
count = 0

while True:

    print("This will run indefinitely.")

    count += 1

    if count >= 3:

        break
```

Output:

This will run indefinitely.

This will run indefinitely.

This will run indefinitely.

Explanation: This while loop will run forever until the break statement is encountered.

4.5 The range() Function

The range() function in Python generates a sequence of numbers, which is typically used in for loops to iterate a specific number of times.

Syntax:

```
range(start, stop, step)
```

- **start**: The value to start the sequence from (default is 0).
- **stop**: The end value (the range will generate numbers up to but not including this value).
- **step**: The increment (default is 1).

Example 1: Using range() with a for loop

```
for i in range(2, 8):
```

```
    print(i)
```

Output:

```
2
3
4
5
6
7
```

Explanation: This example uses range() to generate numbers from 2 to 7.

Example 2: Using range() with step

```
for i in range(1, 10, 2):
    print(i)
```

Output:

```
1
3
5
7
9
```

Explanation: The range() generates numbers from 1 to 9 with a step of 2.

4.6 Loop Control Statements: break, continue, and pass

Python provides three control statements—**break, continue**, and **pass**—to modify the behavior of loops.

4.6.1 break Statement

The break statement terminates the loop prematurely when a specified condition is met.

Example:

```
for i in range(5):
    if i == 3:
        break
    print(i)
```

Output:

```
0
1
2
```

Explanation: The loop stops when i equals 3, and the break statement terminates the loop early.

4.6.2 continue Statement

The continue statement skips the rest of the current iteration and moves to the next iteration of the loop.

Example:

```python
for i in range(5):
    if i == 3:
        continue
    print(i)
```

Output:

```
0
1
2
4
```

Explanation: When i equals 3, the continue statement skips the print statement and moves to the next iteration.

4.6.3 pass Statement

The pass statement is a placeholder that does nothing. It's used when a statement is required syntactically but no action is needed.

Example:

```python
for i in range(5):
    if i == 3:
        pass  # Do nothing
    print(i)
```

Output:

```
0
1
2
3
4
```

Explanation: The loop proceeds as usual, but when i is 3, the pass statement is used, doing nothing.

4.7 Nested Loops

Nested loops are loops within loops. They are used when you need to perform iterative operations on multi-dimensional data structures, such as matrices, or generate combinations of values.

Example 1: Iterating over a matrix

```python
matrix = [
```

```
    [1, 2, 3],

    [4, 5, 6],

    [7, 8, 9]

]

for row in matrix:

    for value in row:

        print(value, end=' ')

    print()
```

Output:

```
1 2 3
4 5 6
7 8 9
```

Explanation: The outer loop iterates over the rows, and the inner loop iterates over each element in the row.

Example 2: Generating combinations

```
colors = ['red', 'green', 'blue']

sizes = ['small', 'medium', 'large']

for color in colors:

    for size in sizes:

        print(f'{size} {color} shirt')
```

Output:

```
small red shirt
medium red shirt
large red shirt
small green shirt
medium green shirt
large green shirt
small blue shirt
medium blue shirt
large blue shirt
```

Explanation: This nested loop generates combinations of colors and sizes.

4.8 Using else in Loops

In Python, you can use an else block with loops. The else block is executed when the loop completes all iterations without encountering a break statement.

Example 1: Using else with a for loop

```python
fruits = ["apple", "banana", "cherry"]

for fruit in fruits:
    print(fruit)
else:
    print("No more fruits left.")
```

Output:

```
apple

banana

cherry

No more fruits left.
```

Explanation: The else block is executed after the loop finishes normally (without a break).

Example 2: Using else with a while loop

```python
count = 0
while count < 5:
    print(count)
    count += 1
else:
    print("Loop completed successfully.")
```

Output:

```
0
1
2
3
4
Loop completed successfully.
```

Explanation: The else block is executed once the while loop terminates successfully.

4.9 Best Practices for Loops

1. **Avoid Infinite Loops**: Ensure that the loop condition will eventually become false to prevent infinite loops.

2. **Use break, continue, and pass wisely**: These control statements can help in efficiently managing loop flow but should be used sparingly to maintain code clarity.

3. **Keep Loop Nesting to a Minimum**: Avoid excessive nesting to ensure the readability and maintainability of your code.

4. **Initialization and Incrementation**: Always ensure proper initialization of loop variables and incrementation/decrementation to achieve the desired results.

4.10 Exercise Questions

1. Write a Python program that prints the numbers from 1 to 10 using a for loop.

2. Write a Python program that uses a while loop to print the first 5 square numbers (1, 4, 9, 16, 25).

3. Complete the following code to print numbers from 5 to 1 using a while loop:

```
count = 5

while count > 0:

    # Code to print count

    count -= 1
```

4. Write a Python program that uses a for loop and the range() function to print all odd numbers between 1 and 20.

5. Find the error in the following code and fix it:

```
for i in range(5)

    print(i)
```

6. Write a Python program that uses a while loop to print the sum of the numbers from 1 to 10.

7. Complete the following code to print a countdown from 10 to 1 using a while loop:

```
count = 10

# Write the loop to print the countdown
```

8. Write a Python program that prints the factorial of a number (5) using a for loop.

9. Find the error in the following code and fix it:

```
x = 0

while x < 5:

    print("x is:", x)
```

```python
    x += 1
else:
    print("Loop ended")
```

10. Write a Python program that uses a for loop to iterate 5 times and prints "Iteration X" for each iteration, where X is the current iteration number.

11. Complete the code to print the numbers 2, 4, 6, 8, 10 using the range() function and a for loop:

```python
for i in range(2, 12, 2):
    # Print i
```

12. Write a Python program that uses a while loop to count and print the number of vowels in the string "Hello, World!".

13. Find the error in the following code and correct it:

```python
for i in range(1, 6):
    if i == 3:
        break
    print(i)
```

14. Write a Python program that uses a while loop to print the numbers from 1 to 100, but only print numbers divisible by 3.

15. Complete the following code to print the first 5 multiples of 4 using a for loop and range():

```python
for i in range(4, 21, 4):
    # Print i
```

Solutions to the Questions

1. Write a Python program that prints the numbers from 1 to 10 using a for loop.

```python
for i in range(1, 11):
    print(i)
```

2. Write a Python program that uses a while loop to print the first 5 square numbers (1, 4, 9, 16, 25).

```python
count = 1
while count <= 5:
    print(count**2)
    count += 1
```

3. Complete the following code to print numbers from 5 to 1 using a while loop:

```
count = 5

while count > 0:

    print(count)

    count -= 1
```

4. Write a Python program that uses a for loop and the range() function to print all odd numbers between 1 and 20.

```
for i in range(1, 21, 2):

    print(i)
```

5. Find the error in the following code and fix it:

```
for i in range(5):  # Add colon at the end of the for statement

    print(i)
```

6. Write a Python program that uses a while loop to print the sum of the numbers from 1 to 10.

```
count = 1

total = 0

while count <= 10:

    total += count

    count += 1

print("Sum:", total)
```

7. Complete the following code to print a countdown from 10 to 1 using a while loop:

```
count = 10

while count > 0:

    print(count)

    count -= 1
```

8. Write a Python program that prints the factorial of a number (5) using a for loop.

```
factorial = 1

for i in range(1, 6):

    factorial *= i

print("Factorial of 5:", factorial)
```

9. Find the error in the following code and fix it:

```
x = 0

while x < 5:
```

```python
    print("x is:", x)

    x += 1

else:

    print("Loop ended")
```

Error: The else block in a loop will only execute if the loop terminates without encountering a break. This code is correct as written, so there's no error here. The output will print x is: 0, then x is: 1, etc., followed by "Loop ended."

10. Write a Python program that uses a for loop to iterate 5 times and print "Iteration X" for each iteration, where X is the current iteration number.

```python
for i in range(1, 6):

    print(f"Iteration {i}")
```

11. Complete the code to print the numbers 2, 4, 6, 8, 10 using the range() function and a for loop:

```python
for i in range(2, 12, 2):

    print(i)
```

12. Write a Python program that uses a while loop to count and print the number of vowels in the string "Hello, World!".

```python
string = "Hello, World!"

vowels = "aeiouAEIOU"

count = 0

index = 0

while index < len(string):

    if string[index] in vowels:

        count += 1

    index += 1

print("Number of vowels:", count)
```

13. Find the error in the following code and correct it:

```python
for i in range(1, 6):

    if i == 3:

        break  # This should break the loop when i equals 3

    print(i)
```

Error: The print(i) statement is unreachable after break because the loop exits early. The code is correct as written, but the output will be 1 2, and the loop will stop when i is 3.

14. Write a Python program that uses a while loop to print the numbers from 1 to 100, but only print numbers divisible by 3.

count = 1

while count <= 100:

    if count % 3 == 0:

        print(count)

    count += 1

15. Complete the following code to print the first 5 multiples of 4 using a for loop and range():

for i in range(4, 21, 4):

    print(i)

4.11 Check your Logic

1. Grocery Store Sales Analysis

Scenario:
A local grocery store wants to analyze its daily sales data. The owner wants a Python program that can:

1. Accept sales data for 7 days as input (one value for each day).
2. Calculate and display the total sales for the week.
3. Find the day with the highest sales and the day with the lowest sales.
4. If the total sales for the week exceed ₹50,000, print "Excellent Sales Week!". Otherwise, print "Room for Improvement."

Requirements:

- Use a for loop to calculate the total sales.
- Use if statements to determine the highest and lowest sales.
- Use appropriate indentation to ensure code readability.

2. Student Grade Processing

Scenario:
A teacher wants to automate the process of assigning grades to students based on their scores in a class test. The grading criteria are as follows:

- 90 and above: Grade A
- 75 to 89: Grade B
- 60 to 74: Grade C
- Below 60: Grade D

Write a Python program that:

1. Accepts the scores of 5 students as input.

2. Uses a for loop to iterate through the scores and assign grades based on the criteria.
3. Prints each student's score along with their grade.
4. At the end, prints the average score of the class.

Requirements:

- Use a for loop to process the scores.
- Use if-elif-else statements to determine the grade.
- Ensure proper use of indentation and control flow.

3. Scenario: Bank ATM Simulation

Scenario:

A bank wants a Python program to simulate an ATM machine. The machine has the following features:

1. A user starts with a balance of ₹10,000.

2. The user can perform three operations:

   a) Withdraw money
   b) Deposit money
   c) Check balance

3. The ATM should allow the user to perform operations in a loop until they choose to exit.

4. The ATM should not allow withdrawals greater than the available balance or deposits greater than ₹50,000 in a single transaction.

5. If the user enters an invalid choice, the program should display "Invalid option, please try again."

Requirements:

- Use a while loop to keep the program running until the user chooses to exit.
- Use if-elif-else statements to handle the user's choices.
- Use proper control flow and loop termination.

4. Scenario: Employee Work Hours Tracker

Scenario:

A company wants a Python program to manage its employees' work hours and calculate overtime pay. Each employee is required to work 40 hours a week, and any extra hours are considered overtime. The program should:

1. Accept the names of 5 employees and their total hours worked for the week.

2. For each employee:

   a) If the hours worked are greater than 40, calculate the overtime pay. Overtime is paid at ₹200 per hour.
   b) If the hours worked are less than 40, calculate the hours short of the requirement.

3. Display the following for each employee:

   a) Name
   b) Total hours worked
   c) Overtime pay or hours short (as applicable)

4. Calculate and display:

    a) The total overtime paid by the company.

    b) The total hours short for all employees combined.

Requirements:

- Use a for loop to process the employees' data.
- Use if-else statements to calculate overtime or hours short.
- Keep the program dynamic, allowing easy adjustments to employee count or pay rates.

5. Scenario: Library Management System

Scenario:

A library wants a Python program to manage its books and transactions. The program should:

1. Allow the librarian to manage a collection of up to 10 books. For each book, store its title and availability status (available or issued).

2. Provide the following features:

    o **View All Books**: Display all books with their availability status.

    o **Issue a Book**: Accept the title of a book from the user. If the book is available, mark it as issued and display "Book Issued." If not, display "Book not available."

    o **Return a Book**: Accept the title of a book from the user. If the book is issued, mark it as available and display "Book Returned." If not, display "Invalid Return."

    o **Add a New Book**: Accept the title of a new book. Add it to the collection if space allows (up to 10 books). If the collection is full, display "Cannot add more books."

    o **Exit**: End the program.

3. Allow the librarian to perform multiple actions in a loop until they choose to exit.

Requirements:

- Use a list to store the collection of books.
- Use a while loop to allow repeated operations.
- Use if-elif-else statements to handle user input and perform the appropriate actions.
- Ensure proper handling of edge cases, such as trying to issue a non-existent book or returning a book not in the collection.

Solution

1. Grocery Store Sales Analysis

```python
# Initialize variables
total_sales = 0
highest_sales = 0
lowest_sales = float('inf')
highest_day = 0
lowest_day = 0
# Accept sales data for 7 days
```

```python
for day in range(1, 8):
    daily_sales = float(input(f"Enter sales for day {day}: ₹"))
    total_sales += daily_sales
    if daily_sales > highest_sales:
        highest_sales = daily_sales
        highest_day = day
    if daily_sales < lowest_sales:
        lowest_sales = daily_sales
        lowest_day = day
# Display results
print(f"\nTotal sales for the week: ₹{total_sales}")
print(f"Highest sales: ₹{highest_sales} on day {highest_day}")
print(f"Lowest sales: ₹{lowest_sales} on day {lowest_day}")
# Check performance
if total_sales > 50000:
    print("Excellent Sales Week!")
else:
    print("Room for Improvement.")
```

2. Student Grade Processing

```python
# Initialize variables
total_score = 0
# Process grades for 5 students
for i in range(1, 6):
    score = int(input(f"Enter the score of student {i}: "))
    total_score += score
    if score >= 90:
        grade = 'A'
    elif score >= 75:
        grade = 'B'
    elif score >= 60:
        grade = 'C'
    else:
        grade = 'D'
    print(f"Student {i} - Score: {score}, Grade: {grade}")
```

```python
# Calculate and display average score
average_score = total_score / 5
print(f"\nAverage score of the class: {average_score:.2f}")
```

3. Bank ATM Simulation

```python
# Initial balance
balance = 10000
while True:
    print("\nATM Menu:")
    print("1. Withdraw Money")
    print("2. Deposit Money")
    print("3. Check Balance")
    print("4. Exit")
    choice = input("Choose an option (1-4): ")
    if choice == '1':  # Withdraw
        amount = float(input("Enter amount to withdraw: ₹"))
        if amount > balance:
            print("Insufficient balance.")
        else:
            balance -= amount
            print(f"Withdrawal successful. Remaining balance: ₹{balance}")
    elif choice == '2':  # Deposit
        amount = float(input("Enter amount to deposit: ₹"))
        if amount > 50000:
            print("Cannot deposit more than ₹50,000 in a single transaction.")
        else:
            balance += amount
            print(f"Deposit successful. Updated balance: ₹{balance}")
    elif choice == '3':  # Check balance
        print(f"Current balance: ₹{balance}")
    elif choice == '4':  # Exit
        print("Thank you for using the ATM. Goodbye!")
        break
    else:
        print("Invalid option, please try again.")
```

4. Employee Work Hours Tracker

```python
# Initialize variables
total_overtime_pay = 0
total_hours_short = 0


# Process data for 5 employees
for i in range(1, 6):
    name = input(f"Enter the name of employee {i}: ")
    hours_worked = int(input(f"Enter total hours worked by {name}: "))
    if hours_worked > 40:
        overtime_hours = hours_worked - 40
        overtime_pay = overtime_hours * 200
        total_overtime_pay += overtime_pay
        print(f"{name} worked {hours_worked} hours with ₹{overtime_pay} overtime pay.")
    elif hours_worked < 40:
        hours_short = 40 - hours_worked
        total_hours_short += hours_short
        print(f"{name} worked {hours_worked} hours and is short by {hours_short} hours.")
    else:
        print(f"{name} worked exactly 40 hours with no overtime or shortfall.")


# Summary
print(f"\nTotal overtime paid by the company: ₹{total_overtime_pay}")
print(f"Total hours short across all employees: {total_hours_short} hours")
```

5. Library Management System

```python
# Initialize variables for book collection
book1 = {"title": "Book 1", "status": "available"}
book2 = {"title": "Book 2", "status": "issued"}
book3 = {"title": "Book 3", "status": "available"}
book_count = 3


def view_books():
    print("\nBooks in the Library:")
    for i, book in enumerate([book1, book2, book3], start=1):
        if i > book_count:
```

```python
        break
    print(f"{book['title']} - {book['status']}")


def issue_book(title):
    for book in [book1, book2, book3]:
        if book["title"] == title:
            if book["status"] == "available":
                book["status"] = "issued"
                print("Book Issued.")
            else:
                print("Book not available.")
            return
    print("Book not found.")


def return_book(title):
    for book in [book1, book2, book3]:
        if book["title"] == title:
            if book["status"] == "issued":
                book["status"] = "available"
                print("Book Returned.")
            else:
                print("Invalid Return.")
            return
    print("Book not found.")


def add_book(title):
    global book_count
    if book_count >= 3:
        print("Cannot add more books.")
    else:
        book_count += 1
        globals()[f"book{book_count}"] = {"title": title, "status": "available"}
        print("Book added to the collection.")


while True:
    print("\nLibrary Menu:")
```

```python
print("1. View All Books")
print("2. Issue a Book")
print("3. Return a Book")
print("4. Add a New Book")
print("5. Exit")
choice = input("Choose an option (1-5): ")

if choice == '1':  # View all books
    view_books()
elif choice == '2':  # Issue a book
    title = input("Enter the title of the book to issue: ")
    issue_book(title)
elif choice == '3':  # Return a book
    title = input("Enter the title of the book to return: ")
    return_book(title)
elif choice == '4':  # Add a new book
    title = input("Enter the title of the new book: ")
    add_book(title)
elif choice == '5':  # Exit
    print("Exiting the library management system. Goodbye!")
    break
else:
    print("Invalid option, please try again.")
```

5. Functions In Python

Functions are essential in Python programming for organizing and structuring code efficiently. They promote code reuse, improve flexibility, and simplify debugging. By encapsulating logic within functions, developers can enhance readability, scalability, and maintainability of Python programs.

5.1 Defining Functions

Functions allow you to encapsulate code logic into reusable blocks. These blocks can be executed by calling the function name, passing arguments if required, and handling the returned output.

Syntax:

```
def function_name(parameters):

    """docstring"""

    # Function body

    # Statements

    return expression
```

- The function_name should follow Python naming conventions, such as using lowercase with underscores.

- Parameters are optional and are placed inside parentheses.

- A docstring is used for describing the function's purpose, inputs, and outputs.

- The return statement is optional but is used when the function needs to return a result.

Example: Greeting Function

```
def greet(name):

    """This function greets the user by their name."""

    print(f"Namaste, {name}!")

# Calling the function

greet("Aarav")
```

Output:

```
Namaste, Aarav!
```

5.2 Function Parameters

Functions can accept zero or more parameters. These parameters allow dynamic inputs during function calls.

Example with Parameters

```
def add_numbers(a, b):

    """This function adds two numbers and returns the result."""
```

```python
    return a + b

# Calling the function

result = add_numbers(15, 20)

print(result)  # Output: 35
```

Example with Default Parameters

```python
def greet(name="Guest"):

    """This function greets the user with a default name if none is provided."""

    print(f"Hello, {name}!")

# Calling the function

greet()  # Output: Hello, Guest!

greet("Rekha")  # Output: Hello, Rekha!
```

5.3 Function Documentation (Docstring)

A docstring provides documentation for a function and is enclosed within triple quotes (""").

Example:

```python
def multiply(a, b):

    """This function multiplies two numbers and returns the result."""

    return a * b

# Accessing the docstring

print(multiply.__doc__)
```

Output:

This function multiplies two numbers and returns the result.

5.4 Return Statement

The return statement allows a function to send back a result to the caller.

Example:

```python
def calculate_square(x):

    """This function calculates the square of a number."""

    return x ** 2
```

```python
# Calling the function
result = calculate_square(7)
print(result)  # Output: 49
```

5.5 Scope of Variables in Functions

Variables defined inside a function are local to that function and cannot be accessed outside unless declared as global.

Example:

```python
def show_product(a, b):
    """This function calculates and displays the product of two numbers."""
    product = a * b  # Local variable
    print(f"The product is: {product}")


# Calling the function
show_product(10, 20)
```

5.6 Lambda Functions

Lambda functions are anonymous, small functions defined using the lambda keyword. They are often used for short operations.

Example:

```python
double = lambda x: x * 2
print(double(10))  # Output: 20
```

5.7 Recursion

Recursion is a technique where a function calls itself to solve smaller instances of a problem.

Example: Factorial Calculation

```python
def factorial(n):
    """This function calculates the factorial of a number."""
    if n == 0:
        return 1
```

```python
    else:
        return n * factorial(n - 1)

# Calling the function

print(factorial(5))  # Output: 120
```

5.8 Variable-Length Arguments

Variable-length arguments allow functions to accept a flexible number of inputs using *args.

Example:

```python
def sum_numbers(*args):
    """This function calculates the sum of a variable number of arguments."""
    total = 0

    for num in args:
        total += num

    return total


# Calling the function

print(sum_numbers(10, 20, 30))  # Output: 60
```

5.9 Inner Functions

An inner function is a function defined inside another function. It provides encapsulation and improves code organization.

Example:

```python
def outer_function(greeting):
    """Outer function demonstrating an inner function."""
    def inner_function(name):
        print(f"{greeting}, {name}!")
    return inner_function


# Creating a closure

closure = outer_function("Hello")

closure("Amit")  # Output: Hello, Amit!
```

5.10 Exercise Questions

1. **Define a function square that takes one parameter and returns its square.**

```python
def square(x):
    """Returns the square of a number."""
    return x ** 2
print(square(5))  # Output: 25
```

2. **Create a function subtract_numbers that takes two parameters and returns their difference.**

```python
def subtract_numbers(a, b):
    """Subtracts b from a and returns the result."""
    return a - b
print(subtract_numbers(15, 5))  # Output: 10
```

3. **Write a function divide with a docstring that explains its purpose, inputs, and return value.**

```python
def divide(a, b):
    """
    Divides a by b and returns the result.
    Parameters:
    a (float): Numerator
    b (float): Denominator
    Returns:
    float: Result of division
    """
    return a / b
print(divide(50, 10))  # Output: 5.0
```

4. **Write a function is_even that takes an integer and returns True if it is even, otherwise False.**

```python
def is_even(n):
    """Returns True if n is even, otherwise False."""
    return n % 2 == 0


print(is_even(10))  # Output: True
```

5. **Write a function product using *args to calculate the product of all arguments.**

```python
def product(*args):
    """Calculates the product of all provided numbers."""
    result = 1
    for num in args:
        result *= num
    return result
print(product(2, 3, 4))  # Output: 24
```

5.11 Chek your Logic

1. Write a function factorial that calculates the factorial of a number using a while loop instead of recursion. Test it by calculating the factorial of 6.

2. Define a function is_prime that takes a number as input and returns True if the number is prime, otherwise False. Use a for loop to check for divisors.

3. Write a Python program that accepts a string and a character as input and uses a function char_count to count how many times the character appears in the string.

4. Create a function greet_names that accepts a list of names and prints a personalized greeting for each name using a for loop.

5. Write a function reverse_digits that takes an integer as input and returns its reverse. For example, input 1234 should return 4321.

6. Define a function max_of_three that takes three numbers as parameters and returns the largest number using nested if-else statements.

7. Create a function check_password that accepts a string as input. The function should return True if the string has at least one uppercase letter, one lowercase letter, and one digit, otherwise return False.

8. Write a Python program that uses a function find_vowels to accept a sentence as input and return a list of all the vowels in the sentence.

9. Create a function multiplication_table that accepts an integer n and prints its multiplication table up to 10 using a for loop.

10. Write a program that uses a function calc_average to calculate the average of a variable number of inputs using *args.

11. Define a function calculate_area that accepts two parameters: the shape (e.g., "circle", "rectangle", "square") and its dimensions. The function should calculate and return the area of the given shape.

12. Write a Python program to find the sum of all odd numbers between 1 and 100. Use a function sum_odd_numbers and a for loop.

13. Create a function grade_students that accepts a list of scores and prints grades for each score based on the following criteria:

- 90 and above: Grade A

- 75 to 89: Grade B

- 60 to 74: Grade C

- Below 60: Grade D

14. Write a function remove_duplicates that accepts a string and returns a new string with all duplicate characters removed. For example, input programming should return progamin.

15. Define a function fibonacci_sequence that accepts an integer n and prints the first n terms of the Fibonacci sequence.

16. Create a function validate_email that accepts an email address as input and checks if it contains '@' and ends with a valid domain like .com, .in, or .org. Return True if valid, otherwise return False.

17. Write a Python program that uses a function digit_sum to calculate the sum of the digits of an integer. For example, input 123 should return 6.

18. Create a function even_odd_sum that takes a list of integers and returns two values: the sum of even numbers and the sum of odd numbers.

19. Write a function pattern_printer that accepts an integer n and prints a right-angled triangle pattern of * with n rows. For example, for n = 3:

*

**

***

20. Define a function palindrome_check that accepts a string and checks if it is a palindrome (reads the same forward and backward). Return True if it is a palindrome, otherwise return False.

Solutions:

1. **Factorial using a while loop**

```python
def factorial(n):
    """Calculates factorial using a while loop."""
    result = 1
    while n > 0:
        result *= n
        n -= 1
    return result


print(factorial(6))  # Output: 720
```

2. **Prime Number Check**

```python
def is_prime(num):
    """Checks if a number is prime."""
    if num < 2:
        return False
    for i in range(2, num):
        if num % i == 0:
            return False
    return True
print(is_prime(11))  # Output: True
print(is_prime(9))   # Output: False
```

3. **Count Character in a String**

```python
def char_count(string, char):
    """Counts occurrences of a character in a string."""
    count = 0
    for c in string:
        if c == char:
            count += 1
    return count


print(char_count("programming", "m"))  # Output: 2
```

4. **Greeting Multiple Names**

```python
def greet_names(names):
    """Greets each name in the list."""
    for name in names:
        print(f"Hello, {name}!")


greet_names(["Aarav", "Rekha", "Meera"])
```

5. **Reverse Digits of an Integer**

```python
def reverse_digits(num):
    """Reverses the digits of an integer."""
    reversed_num = 0
    while num > 0:
        digit = num % 10
        reversed_num = reversed_num * 10 + digit
```

```python
        num = num // 10
    return reversed_num


print(reverse_digits(1234))  # Output: 4321
```

6. **Maximum of Three Numbers**

```python
def max_of_three(a, b, c):
    """Finds the maximum of three numbers."""
    if a > b:
        if a > c:
            return a
        else:
            return c
    else:
        if b > c:
            return b
        else:
            return c


print(max_of_three(10, 20, 15))  # Output: 20
```

7. **Password Validation**

```python
def check_password(password):
    """Validates a password based on character types."""
    has_upper = False
    has_lower = False
    has_digit = False

    for char in password:
        if 'A' <= char <= 'Z':
            has_upper = True
        if 'a' <= char <= 'z':
            has_lower = True
        if '0' <= char <= '9':
            has_digit = True

    if has_upper and has_lower and has_digit:
        return True
```

```python
    else:
        return False

print(check_password("Password123"))  # Output: True
print(check_password("password"))     # Output: False
```

8. **Find Vowels in a Sentence**

```python
def find_vowels(sentence):
    """Finds all vowels in a sentence."""
    vowels = "aeiouAEIOU"
    result = []
    for char in sentence:
        if char in vowels:
            result.append(char)
    return result

print(find_vowels("Hello World"))  # Output: ['e', 'o', 'o']
```

9. **Multiplication Table**

```python
def multiplication_table(n):
    """Prints the multiplication table of n."""
    for i in range(1, 11):
        print(f"{n} x {i} = {n * i}")

multiplication_table(5)
```

10. **Calculate Average using *args**

```python
def calc_average(*args):
    """Calculates the average of variable inputs."""
    total = 0
    count = 0
    for num in args:
        total += num
        count += 1
    if count == 0:
        return 0
    return total / count

print(calc_average(10, 20, 30, 40))  # Output: 25.0
```

11. **Calculate Area Based on Shape**

```python
def calculate_area(shape, *dimensions):
    """Calculates area of the given shape."""
    if shape == "circle":
        radius = dimensions[0]
        return 3.14 * radius * radius
    elif shape == "rectangle":
        length = dimensions[0]
        breadth = dimensions[1]
        return length * breadth
    elif shape == "square":
        side = dimensions[0]
        return side * side
    else:
        return "Invalid shape"


print(calculate_area("circle", 7))  # Output: 153.86
print(calculate_area("rectangle", 5, 10))  # Output: 50
```

12. **Sum of Odd Numbers from 1 to 100**

```python
def sum_odd_numbers():
    """Calculates the sum of odd numbers between 1 and 100."""
    total = 0
    for num in range(1, 101):
        if num % 2 != 0:
            total += num
    return total


print(sum_odd_numbers())  # Output: 2500
```

13. **Grading Students**

```python
def grade_students(scores):
    """Assigns grades based on scores."""
    for score in scores:
        if score >= 90:
            grade = "A"
        elif score >= 75:
            grade = "B"
```

```python
    elif score >= 60:
        grade = "C"
    else:
        grade = "D"
    print(f"Score: {score}, Grade: {grade}")


grade_students([95, 82, 68, 55])
```

14.   Remove Duplicates from a String

```python
def remove_duplicates(string):
    """Removes duplicate characters from a string."""
    result = ""
    for char in string:
        if char not in result:
            result += char
    return result


print(remove_duplicates("programming"))  # Output: progamin
```

15.   Fibonacci Sequence

```python
def fibonacci_sequence(n):
    """Prints the first n terms of the Fibonacci sequence."""
    a, b = 0, 1
    for _ in range(n):
        print(a, end=" ")
        a, b = b, a + b


fibonacci_sequence(7)  # Output: 0 1 1 2 3 5 8
```

16.   Email Validation

```python
def validate_email(email):
    """Validates if the email contains '@' and ends with a valid domain."""
    valid_domains = [".com", ".in", ".org"]

    if "@" not in email:
        return False

    for domain in valid_domains:
        if email.endswith(domain):
```

```python
        return True
    return False
print(validate_email("test@example.com"))  # Output: True
print(validate_email("test@example"))     # Output: False
```

17. **Sum of Digits of an Integer**

```python
def digit_sum(num):
    """Calculates the sum of the digits of an integer."""
    total = 0
    while num > 0:
        total += num % 10
        num //= 10
    return total


print(digit_sum(123))  # Output: 6
```

18. **Even and Odd Sum from a List**

```python
def even_odd_sum(numbers):
    """Returns the sum of even and odd numbers from the list."""
    even_sum = 0
    odd_sum = 0
    for num in numbers:
        if num % 2 == 0:
            even_sum += num
        else:
            odd_sum += num
    return even_sum, odd_sum


print(even_odd_sum([1, 2, 3, 4, 5, 6]))  # Output: (12, 9)
```

19. **Print a Pattern**

```python
def pattern_printer(n):
    """Prints a right-angled triangle pattern of '*'."""
    for i in range(1, n+1):
        print('*' * i)


pattern_printer(3)
# Output:
```

```
# *
# **
# ***
```

20. **Palindrome Check**

```python
def palindrome_check(string):
    """Checks if the string is a palindrome."""
    reversed_string = ""
    for char in string:
        reversed_string = char + reversed_string
    if string == reversed_string:
        return True
    else:
        return False


print(palindrome_check("madam"))  # Output: True
print(palindrome_check("hello"))  # Output: False
```

6. Strings in Python

In Python, strings are sequences of characters used for storing and manipulating text. They are one of the most versatile and commonly used data types, offering numerous operations and methods for text handling. This chapter explores the basics of Python strings, their operations, slicing, concatenation, and more, enriched with examples relevant to Indian contexts.

6.1 Creating Strings

Strings in Python can be created using single quotes, double quotes, or triple quotes.

Single quotes are best for simple strings that do not contain single quotes. For instance:

```
greeting = 'Namaste!'

print(greeting)  # Output: Namaste!
```

If a single quote needs to appear in the string, it must be escaped with a backslash:

```
sentence = 'It\'s a sunny day in Jaipur.'

print(sentence)  # Output: It's a sunny day in Jaipur.
```

Double quotes help when single quotes need to be included without escaping:

```
quote = "It's a great time for chai and samosas."

print(quote)  # Output: It's a great time for chai and samosas.
```

Triple quotes are used for multi-line strings or when both single and double quotes are present. They also preserve line breaks:

```
festival = """India is known for its festivals.

Diwali is a festival of lights celebrated with great joy."""

print(festival)

# Output:

# India is known for its festivals.

# Diwali is a festival of lights celebrated with great joy.
```

They also allow strings with both single and double quotes:

```
mixed_quotes = '''She said, "It's a lovely day in Kerala!"'''

print(mixed_quotes) # Output: She said, "It's a lovely day in Kerala!"
```

6.2 Accessing Characters in a String

Strings in Python are indexed arrays, allowing characters to be accessed using their position.

Positive indexing starts from 0. For example:

```python
city = "Mumbai"

print(city[0])  # Output: M

print(city[1])  # Output: u
```

Negative indexing starts from -1, making it useful for accessing characters from the end:

```python
city = "Kolkata"

print(city[-1])  # Output: a

print(city[-2])  # Output: t
```

Mixed indexing combines positive and negative indexing:

```python
phrase = "Incredible India"

print(phrase[0])   # Output: I

print(phrase[-1])  # Output: a
```

Trying to access an out-of-range index raises an IndexError:

```python
word = "Delhi"

print(word[10])  # Raises IndexError
```

6.3 Slicing Strings

String slicing extracts parts of a string using the syntax string[start:stop:step]. For example:

```python
state = "Tamil Nadu"

print(state[0:5])  # Output: Tamil

print(state[:5])   # Output: Tamil

print(state[6:])   # Output: Nadu
```

Negative indices allow slicing from the end:

```python
state = "West Bengal"

print(state[-6:])  # Output: Bengal
```

Skipping parameters uses default values:

```python
state = "Uttar Pradesh"

print(state[:])    # Output: Uttar Pradesh

print(state[::2])  # Output: UtrPdeh
```

A negative step reverses the slice:

```python
name = "Kerala"

print(name[::-1])  # Output: alareK
```

6.4 String Concatenation

Concatenation combines strings into one. The + operator is the simplest method:

```python
part1 = "India"

part2 = "is great!"

result = part1 + " " + part2

print(result)  # Output: India is great!
```

The join() method joins elements from a list:

```python
states = ["Punjab", "Haryana", "Himachal"]

result = ", ".join(states)

print(result)  # Output: Punjab, Haryana, Himachal
```

Formatted string literals (f-strings) allow embedding variables directly:

```python
state = "Rajasthan"

temperature = 40

result = f"The temperature in {state} is {temperature}°C."

print(result)  # Output: The temperature in Rajasthan is 40°C.
```

The format() method works similarly:

```python
city = "Chennai"

population = "7 million"

result = "The population of {} is {}.".format(city, population)

print(result)  # Output: The population of Chennai is 7 million.
```

6.5 String Multiplication

String multiplication repeats a string multiple times. For example:

```python
repeat = "Namaste! " * 3

print(repeat)  # Output: Namaste! Namaste! Namaste!
```

This is useful for creating patterns:

```python
separator = "=" * 30

print(separator)

# Output: ==============================
```

It can also be combined with slicing:

```python
text = "India " * 4

print(text[:10])  # Output: India Indi
```

String multiplication is helpful for visual separators, patterns, or aligning text in outputs.

6.6 String Methods

Python provides a variety of built-in string methods. Here are some of the most commonly used:

len(): Returns the length of the string.

```python
example_string = "Hello, World!"

print(len(example_string))  # Output: 13
```

str.lower(): Converts all characters to lowercase.

```python
example_string = "Hello, World!"

print(example_string.lower())  # Output: 'hello, world!'
```

str.upper(): Converts all characters to uppercase.

```python
example_string = "Hello, World!"

print(example_string.upper())  # Output: 'HELLO, WORLD!'
```

str.strip(): Removes leading and trailing whitespace.

```python
example_string = "  Hello, World!   "

print(example_string.strip())  # Output: 'Hello, World!'
```

str.replace(): Replaces all occurrences of a substring with another substring.

```python
example_string = "Hello, World!"

print(example_string.replace("World", "Python"))  # Output: 'Hello, Python!'
```

str.split(): Splits the string into a list of substrings based on a delimiter.

```python
example_string = "Hello, World!"

print(example_string.split(", "))  # Output: ['Hello', 'World!']
```

str.join(): Joins a list of strings into a single string with a specified delimiter.

```python
string_list = ["Hello", "World"]

delimiter = ", "

joined_string = delimiter.join(string_list)

print(joined_string)  # Output: 'Hello, World'
```

str.find(): Returns the index of the first occurrence of a substring, or -1 if not found.

```python
example_string = "Hello, World!"
```

```python
print(example_string.find("World"))  # Output: 7
```

str.startswith(): Checks if the string starts with a specified substring.

```python
example_string = "Hello, World!"

print(example_string.startswith("Hello"))  # Output: True
```

str.endswith(): Checks if the string ends with a specified substring.

```python
example_string = "Hello, World!"

print(example_string.endswith("World!"))  # Output: True
```

6.7 String Formatting

Old-Style String Formatting

Using the % operator.

```python
name = "Alice"

age = 30

formatted_string = "My name is %s and I am %d years old." % (name, age)

print(formatted_string)  # Output: 'My name is Alice and I am 30 years old.'
```

str.format() Method

```python
name = "Alice"

age = 30

formatted_string = "My name is {} and I am {} years old.".format(name, age)

print(formatted_string)  # Output: 'My name is Alice and I am 30 years old.'
```

f-Strings (Python 3.6+)

```python
name = "Alice"

age = 30

formatted_string = f"My name is {name} and I am {age} years old."

print(formatted_string)  # Output: 'My name is Alice and I am 30 years old.'
```

6.8 Escape Characters

Special characters in strings can be escaped using the backslash (\) character.

- \n - Newline
- \t - Tab
- \' - Single quote
- \" - Double quote

- \\ - Backslash

```python
example_string = "Hello,\nWorld!"

print(example_string)  # Output: 'Hello,
                       #          World!'
```

6.9 Raw Strings

Raw strings ignore escape sequences, making them useful for regular expressions and file paths.

```python
raw_string = r"C:\Users\Name"

print(raw_string)  # Output: 'C:\Users\Name'
```

6.10 String Immutability

Strings in Python are immutable, meaning they cannot be changed after creation. Any modification creates a new string.

```python
example_string = "Hello"

example_string[0] = "h"  # This will raise a TypeError
```

6.11 String Operations

Concatenation: Combining two or more strings.

```python
string1 = "Hello"

string2 = "World"

result = string1 + " " + string2

print(result)  # Output: 'Hello World'
```

Repetition: Repeating a string multiple times.

```python
string = "Hello"

result = string * 3

print(result)  # Output: 'HelloHelloHello'
```

Membership: Checking if a substring exists within a string.

```python
string = "Hello, World!"

print("World" in string)  # Output: True

print("Python" in string)  # Output: False
```

6.12 String Comparison

In Python, strings can be compared using comparison operators, just like numerical values. The comparison is done lexicographically, meaning that the strings are compared character by character based on their Unicode values.

Comparison Operators

The main comparison operators used with strings are:

a. == (equal to)

b. != (not equal to)

c. < (less than)

d. > (greater than)

e. <= (less than or equal to)

f. >= (greater than or equal to)

Lexicographical Comparison

Lexicographical comparison means that strings are compared character by character using their Unicode values. If the characters at the current position are equal, the comparison moves to the next position.

Examples of String Comparison

i. **Equality Comparison**

string1 = "Hello"

string2 = "World"

print(string1 == string2) # Output: False

In this example string1 and string2 are not equal, so the output is False.

ii. **Inequality Comparison**

string1 = "Hello"

string2 = "World"

print(string1 != string2) # Output: True

In this example string1 and string2 are not equal, so the output is True.

iii. **Less Than Comparison**

string1 = "Hello"

string2 = "World"

print(string1 < string2) # Output: True

In this example string1 is considered less than string2 lexicographically because the Unicode value of 'H' is less than 'W'.

iv. **Greater Than Comparison**

string1 = "Hello"

string2 = "Apple"

print(string1 > string2) # Output: True

In this example string1 is considered greater than string2 lexicographically because the Unicode value of 'H' is greater than 'A'.

v.   Less Than or Equal To Comparison

string1 = "Hello"

string2 = "Hello"

print(string1 <= string2) # Output: True

In this example string1 is equal to string2, so the output is True.

vi.   Greater Than or Equal To Comparison

string1 = "Hello"

string2 = "Hell"

print(string1 >= string2) # Output: True

In this example string1 is considered greater than string2 because it has an additional character 'o' at the end.

Case Sensitivity in String Comparison

String comparison in Python is case-sensitive by default. This means that uppercase and lowercase characters are considered different.

Example

string1 = "hello"

string2 = "Hello"

print(string1 == string2) # Output: False

In this example the lowercase 'h' is not equal to the uppercase 'H', so the output is False.

Ignoring Case in Comparison

To compare strings without considering case, you can convert both strings to the same case using the lower() or upper() methods.

Example

string1 = "hello"

string2 = "Hello"

print(string1.lower() == string2.lower()) # Output: True

In this example both strings are converted to lowercase before comparison, resulting in True.

6.13 Exercise Questions

1.   Write a Python program to create a string using single quotes and double quotes. Include the text: It's raining in Mumbai.

2.   Create a multi-line string using triple quotes that describes your favorite Indian festival. Print the string to the console.

3.   Access and print the first, third, and last characters from the string "Kolkata".

4.   Given the string "Incredible India", write a program to extract and print:

   a) The substring "Incredible".
   b) The substring "India".
   c) The entire string in reverse order.

5.   Debug the following code and correct the errors to get the output "Tamil Nadu":

state = "TamilNadu"

print(state[:5] + " " state[5:])

6.   Extract every second character from the string "Bengaluru" using slicing.

7.   Write a program to slice and print the string "Kerala" using negative indices.

8.   Concatenate the strings "India", "is", and "beautiful" using:
   a) The + operator.
   b) The join() method.

9.   Debug the following code to correct the string concatenation errors:

city = "Delhi"

message = "The capital of India is " + city "."

print(message)

10.   Create a pattern using string multiplication to display the following output:

****

****

****

11.   Debug the following code to produce the desired repeated output "Namaste Namaste Namaste":

greeting = "Namaste"

print(greeting * 3 + " ")

12.   Given the string "Chennai", write a program to:
   a) Count the number of characters.
   b) Check if the string contains the substring "nn".

13.   Write a Python program to check whether the string "Hyderabad" is a palindrome (ignoring case).

14. Replace all occurrences of the letter 'a' with '@' in the string "Jaipur".

15. The following code is meant to print the substring "Luck". Identify and correct the errors:

city = "Lucknow"

print(city[1:4])

16. Debug the following code to ensure it runs without errors and prints "Hello, World!":

greeting = 'Hello,

World!'

print(greeting)

17. The program is supposed to reverse the string "Goa", but it throws an error. Find and fix the bug:

state = "Goa"

print(state[::-0])

18. Write a Python program to extract the initials of a name entered in the format "First Middle Last". For example, for the input "Mahatma Mohandas Gandhi", the output should be "MMG".

19. Given the string "Maharashtra", write a program to replace all vowels with '*'.

20. The string "Punjab" is accidentally entered as "Punab". Write a program to debug this and insert the missing 'j' at the correct position.

Solution

1. **Program to create a string using single quotes and double quotes:**

Using single quotes

single_quote_string = 'It\'s raining in Mumbai.'

print(single_quote_string)

Using double quotes

double_quote_string = "It's raining in Mumbai."

print(double_quote_string)

2. **Multi-line string using triple quotes:**

favorite_festival = """My favorite festival is Diwali.

It is celebrated with lights, sweets, and fireworks.

Families come together to celebrate the triumph of good over evil."""

print(favorite_festival)

3. **Access and print specific characters from the string "Kolkata":**

city = "Kolkata"

```python
print(city[0])  # First character
print(city[2])  # Third character
print(city[-1])  # Last character
```

4. **Extract and print substrings from "Incredible India":**

```python
phrase = "Incredible India"
print(phrase[:10])  # "Incredible"
print(phrase[11:])  # "India"
print(phrase[::-1])  # Reverse the string
```

5. **Debug and correct the errors to output "Tamil Nadu":**

```python
state = "TamilNadu"
print(state[:5] + " " + state[5:])
```

6. **Extract every second character from "Bengaluru":**

```python
city = "Bengaluru"
print(city[::2])
```

7. **Slice and print the string "Kerala" using negative indices:**

```python
state = "Kerala"
print(state[-6:])  # Full string using negative indices
print(state[-3:])  # Last 3 characters
```

8. **Concatenate the strings "India", "is", and "beautiful":**

```python
# Using +
print("India" + " " + "is" + " " + "beautiful")
# Using join()
words = ["India", "is", "beautiful"]
print(" ".join(words))
```

9. **Debug and correct the string concatenation errors:**

```python
city = "Delhi"
message = "The capital of India is " + city + "."
print(message)
```

10. **Create a pattern using string multiplication:**

```python
pattern = ("*" * 8 + "\n") * 3
```

```
print(pattern)
```

11. **Debug the code to produce "Namaste Namaste Namaste":**

```
greeting = "Namaste"

print((greeting + " ") * 3)
```

12. **Perform operations on the string "Chennai":**

```
city = "Chennai"

# Count characters

print(len(city))

# Check for substring

print("nn" in city)
```

13. **Check if "Hyderabad" is a palindrome (ignoring case):**

```
city = "Hyderabad"

city_lower = city.lower()

print(city_lower == city_lower[::-1])
```

14. **Replace all occurrences of 'a' with '@' in "Jaipur":**

```
city = "Jaipur"

print(city.replace('a', '@'))
```

15. **Debug the code to print "Luck":**

```
city = "Lucknow"

print(city[:4])  # Correct slicing
```

16. **Debug the code to print "Hello, World!":**

```
greeting = 'Hello, \nWorld!'

print(greeting)
```

17. **Debug the code to reverse "Goa":**

```
state = "Goa"

print(state[::-1])
```

18. **Extract initials from a name in the format "First Middle Last":**

```
name = "Mahatma Mohandas Gandhi"

name_parts = name.split()

initials = "".join([part[0].upper() for part in name_parts])
```

```
print(initials)
```

19. **Replace all vowels with '*' in "Maharashtra":**

```
state = "Maharashtra"

vowels = "aeiouAEIOU"

for vowel in vowels:

    state = state.replace(vowel, '*')

print(state)
```

20. **Debug and insert the missing 'j' in "Punab":**

```
state = "Punab"

corrected_state = state[:2] + "j" + state[2:]

print(corrected_state)
```

Scenario-Based Questions

Question 1: Flight Announcement System

A small airport in India uses Python for its flight announcement system. Write a program that accepts the following details from the user:

- Flight number (e.g., "AI101")

- Departure city (e.g., "Delhi")

- Arrival city (e.g., "Mumbai")

- Departure time (e.g., "10:30 AM")

- Arrival time (e.g., "12:45 PM")

The program should display the following message:

"Flight AI101 from Delhi to Mumbai will depart at 10:30 AM and arrive at 12:45 PM."

Additionally, write logic to validate the inputs:
a) Ensure the flight number starts with "AI".
b) Check that the departure and arrival cities are not the same.

Question 2: Personalized Invitation Card Generator

You are tasked with designing a program for an event management company to generate personalized invitation cards for weddings. The program should:

1. Accept the couple's names (e.g., "Aarav" and "Ananya").

2. Accept the event date (e.g., "15th January 2024").

3. Accept the venue details (e.g., "The Taj Mahal Palace, Mumbai").

The program should create a multi-line invitation card in the following format:

Dear Guest,

You are cordially invited to the wedding of Aarav and Ananya.

Date: 15th January 2024

Venue: The Taj Mahal Palace, Mumbai

We look forward to celebrating this joyous occasion with you.

Warm regards,

Event Organizers

The card must preserve the formatting and line breaks exactly as shown.

Question 3: Word Puzzle Validator

A school in Chennai is organizing a word puzzle contest. Participants are given a base word (e.g., "Chennai") and must form smaller words using their letters. Write a Python program that:

1. Takes the base word as input.

2. Accepts a new word from the participant.

3. Validates that the new word only uses letters from the base word.

For example:

- Base word: "Chennai"

- Participant's word: "Chain" -> Valid

- Participant's word: "Rice" -> Invalid (contains letters not in "Chennai")

The program should display appropriate messages for valid and invalid inputs.

Question 4: Dynamic Nameplate Generator

A temple in Tamil Nadu wants to generate dynamic digital nameplates for its donors. Write a Python program that:

1. Accepts the donor's full name (e.g., "Ravi Shankar").

2. Accepts the donation amount (e.g., "₹10,000").

3. Generates and displays the nameplate in the following format:

```
----------------------------------

    Ravi Shankar

  Thank You for Donating

      ₹10,000

----------------------------------
```

The program must handle the alignment of text properly using string multiplication and slicing.

Question 5: Historical Quote Formatter

The government is creating an educational app featuring famous Indian quotes. Write a program that accepts:

1. A quote (e.g., "An eye for an eye will make the whole world blind.").

2. The person who said it (e.g., "Mahatma Gandhi").

The program should output the formatted quote as:


```
"An eye for an eye will make the whole world blind."

        - Mahatma Gandhi
```


Ensure that the speaker's name is right-aligned with the quote by calculating and adding the necessary spaces dynamically.

7. Lists

Lists in Python are one of the most versatile data structures, offering a mutable, ordered collection of elements that can store different data types. They are essential for efficient data manipulation and are widely used in various programming applications. This chapter explores Python lists in detail, with examples relevant to the Indian context.

7.1 Introduction to Lists

A list in Python is a dynamic and mutable collection of elements, allowing additions, deletions, and modifications after creation. Lists maintain the order of elements, making them ideal for scenarios requiring sequence preservation, such as maintaining a list of cities visited on a trip.

For instance:

```python
cities = ["Mumbai", "Delhi", "Bangalore", "Chennai"]

print(cities)

# Output: ['Mumbai', 'Delhi', 'Bangalore', 'Chennai']
```

7.2 Creating Lists

Python provides several ways to create lists, tailored to specific use cases.

7.2.1 Using Square Brackets

Square brackets are the simplest method to define lists.

```python
# A list of famous Indian monuments

monuments = ["Taj Mahal", "Qutub Minar", "Gateway of India"]

print(monuments)

# Output: ['Taj Mahal', 'Qutub Minar', 'Gateway of India']
```

7.2.2 Using the list() Constructor

The list() function converts iterables such as tuples or strings into lists.

```python
# From a tuple

states = list(("Kerala", "Punjab", "Gujarat"))

print(states)

# Output: ['Kerala', 'Punjab', 'Gujarat']

# From a string

characters = list("Namaste")

print(characters)

# Output: ['N', 'a', 'm', 'a', 's', 't', 'e']
```

7.2.3 Mixed Data Types in Lists

Lists can contain multiple data types, offering flexibility in applications.

Mixed data types: name, age, and city

person = ["Aarav", 25, "Hyderabad"]

print(person)

Output: ['Aarav', 25, 'Hyderabad']

7.3 Accessing Elements in a List

Python lists support both positive and negative indexing.

7.3.1 Positive Indexing

Positive indexing starts at 0 for the first element.

languages = ["Hindi", "English", "Tamil", "Bengali"]

print(languages[0]) # Output: 'Hindi'

print(languages[2]) # Output: 'Tamil'

7.3.2 Negative Indexing

Negative indexing begins at -1 for the last element.

languages = ["Hindi", "English", "Tamil", "Bengali"]

print(languages[-1]) # Output: 'Bengali'

print(languages[-3]) # Output: 'English'

7.3.3 Out-of-Range Index

Accessing an index beyond the list length raises an IndexError.

languages = ["Hindi", "English"]

print(languages[5]) # Raises IndexError: list index out of range

7.4 Slicing Lists

Slicing extracts subsets of elements using list[start:stop:step].

7.4.1 Examples of Slicing

states = ["Punjab", "Goa", "Assam", "Odisha", "Karnataka"]

Slice first three states

print(states[:3]) # Output: ['Punjab', 'Goa', 'Assam']

Slice last three states

print(states[-3:]) # Output: ['Assam', 'Odisha', 'Karnataka']

```python
# Reverse the list
print(states[::-1])  # Output: ['Karnataka', 'Odisha', 'Assam', 'Goa', 'Punjab']
```

7.5 Modifying Lists

Lists are mutable, enabling direct modification of their elements.

7.5.1 Changing Elements

```python
festivals = ["Diwali", "Holi", "Eid"]
festivals[1] = "Pongal"
print(festivals)
# Output: ['Diwali', 'Pongal', 'Eid']
```

7.5.2 Adding Elements

```python
festivals.append("Christmas")
print(festivals)
# Output: ['Diwali', 'Pongal', 'Eid', 'Christmas']
```

7.5.3 Removing Elements

```python
festivals.remove("Eid")
print(festivals)
# Output: ['Diwali', 'Pongal', 'Christmas']
```

7.6 List Methods

Lists come with built-in methods to simplify operations.

7.6.1 Sorting and Reversing

```python
numbers = [42, 23, 56, 78, 12]
numbers.sort()
print(numbers)  # Output: [12, 23, 42, 56, 78]
numbers.reverse()
print(numbers)  # Output: [78, 56, 42, 23, 12]
```

7.6.2 Counting and Finding Index

```python
players = ["Sachin", "Virat", "Dhoni", "Sachin"]
print(players.count("Sachin"))  # Output: 2
print(players.index("Dhoni"))  # Output: 2
```

7.7 List Comprehensions

List comprehensions offer a concise way to create lists.

7.7.1 Example: Squares of Numbers

squares = [x**2 for x in range(1, 6)]

print(squares) # Output: [1, 4, 9, 16, 25]

7.7.2 Example: Filtering States by Length

states = ["UP", "Delhi", "Kerala", "Goa"]

short_states = [state for state in states if len(state) <= 3]

print(short_states) # Output: ['UP', 'Goa']

7.8 Nested Lists

Nested lists store hierarchical or multi-dimensional data.

7.8.1 Example: Representing a Matrix

matrix = [[1, 2, 3], [4, 5, 6], [7, 8, 9]]

print(matrix[1][2]) # Output: 6

7.9 Copying Lists

7.9.1 Shallow Copy

original = ["Red", "Green", "Blue"]

copy_list = original.copy()

copy_list[0] = "Yellow"

print(original) # Output: ['Red', 'Green', 'Blue']

print(copy_list) # Output: ['Yellow', 'Green', 'Blue']

7.9.2 Deep Copy

Use the copy module for deep copying.

import copy

nested = [[1, 2], [3, 4]]

deep_copy = copy.deepcopy(nested)

nested[0][0] = 100

print(nested) # Output: [[100, 2], [3, 4]]

print(deep_copy) # Output: [[1, 2], [3, 4]]

7.10 Iterating Through Lists

7.10.1 Using for Loop

states = ["Maharashtra", "Bihar", "West Bengal"]

for state in states:

```
print(state)
```

7.10.2 Using enumerate()

for index, state in enumerate(states):

```
print(f"{index}: {state}")
```

7.11 Exercise Questions

1. Write a Python program to create a list of Indian states. Replace the second state in the list with "Kerala" and then print the updated list.

   states = ["Maharashtra", "Tamil Nadu", "Karnataka"]

   states[1] = "Kerala"

   print(states)

   # Output: ['Maharashtra', 'Kerala', 'Karnataka']

2. Given a list of cities ["Delhi", "Mumbai", "Kolkata", "Chennai", "Bangalore"], write a program to:

   i.   Access and print the first city using positive indexing.

   ii. Access and print the last city using negative indexing.

   cities = ["Delhi", "Mumbai", "Kolkata", "Chennai", "Bangalore"]

   print(cities[0]) # Output: Delhi

   print(cities[-1]) # Output: Bangalore

3. Create a list of famous Indian monuments and slice it to extract:
   a) The first three monuments.
   b) The last two monuments.

   monuments = ["Taj Mahal", "Qutub Minar", "Gateway of India", "Charminar", "India Gate"]

   print(monuments[:3]) # Output: ['Taj Mahal', 'Qutub Minar', 'Gateway of India']

   print(monuments[-2:]) # Output: ['Charminar', 'India Gate']

4. Write a Python program to reverse the list ["Mysore", "Hyderabad", "Jaipur", "Ahmedabad", "Pune"] and print the result.

   cities = ["Mysore", "Hyderabad", "Jaipur", "Ahmedabad", "Pune"]

   print(cities[::-1]) # Output: ['Pune', 'Ahmedabad', 'Jaipur', 'Hyderabad', 'Mysore']

5. Generate a list of even numbers between 1 and 20 using a list comprehension. Print the resulting list.

```python
evens = [x for x in range(1, 21) if x % 2 == 0]

print(evens)  # Output: [2, 4, 6, 8, 10, 12, 14, 16, 18, 20]
```

6. Create a nested list representing a 2x3 matrix (two rows and three columns). Access and print the element in the second row and third column.

```python
matrix = [[1, 2, 3], [4, 5, 6]]

print(matrix[1][2])  # Output: 6
```

7. Given a list of numbers [10, 15, 20, 25, 30, 35, 40], use a list comprehension to create a new list containing only the numbers greater than 20.

```python
numbers = [10, 15, 20, 25, 30, 35, 40]

filtered = [num for num in numbers if num > 20]

print(filtered)  # Output: [25, 30, 35, 40]
```

8. Write a program to find the maximum and minimum numbers in the list [42, 56, 12, 89, 33, 90, 15].

```python
numbers = [42, 56, 12, 89, 33, 90, 15]

print(max(numbers))  # Output: 90

print(min(numbers))  # Output: 12
```

9. Write a Python program to sort the list of scores [76, 89, 45, 92, 58, 73] in descending order without using the sort() method.

```python
scores = [76, 89, 45, 92, 58, 73]

sorted_scores = sorted(scores, reverse=True)

print(sorted_scores)  # Output: [92, 89, 76, 73, 58, 45]
```

10. Create a nested list representing three Indian cities and their corresponding populations. Perform a deep copy of the list, modify the population of one city in the copied list, and print both the original and modified lists to demonstrate independence.

```python
import copy

cities = [["Mumbai", 20000000], ["Delhi", 18000000], ["Chennai", 10000000]]

copied_cities = copy.deepcopy(cities)

copied_cities[0][1] = 22000000

print(cities)  # Output: [['Mumbai', 20000000], ['Delhi', 18000000], ['Chennai', 10000000]]

print(copied_cities)  # Output: [['Mumbai', 22000000], ['Delhi', 18000000], ['Chennai', 10000000]]
```

11. Given two lists of Indian states:
```python
list1 = ["Maharashtra", "Punjab", "Goa", "Kerala"]
list2 = ["Goa", "Kerala", "Rajasthan", "Assam"]
```
Write a Python program to find the common states between the two lists.

```python
list1 = ["Maharashtra", "Punjab", "Goa", "Kerala"]

list2 = ["Goa", "Kerala", "Rajasthan", "Assam"]

common_states = [state for state in list1 if state in list2]

print(common_states)  # Output: ['Goa', 'Kerala']
```

12.   Create a list of cricket players' names where some names are repeated. Write a Python program to count the occurrences of each player's name in the list.

```python
players = ["Sachin", "Virat", "Dhoni", "Sachin", "Virat", "Rohit"]

occurrences = {player: players.count(player) for player in set(players)}

print(occurrences)  # Output: {'Rohit': 1, 'Virat': 2, 'Dhoni': 1, 'Sachin': 2}
```

13.   Write a Python program to add two 2x2 matrices represented as nested lists.

```python
matrix_a = [[1, 2], [3, 4]]

matrix_b = [[5, 6], [7, 8]]

result = [[matrix_a[i][j] + matrix_b[i][j] for j in range(2)] for i in range(2)]

print(result)  # Output: [[6, 8], [10, 12]]
```

14.   Given a list of famous Indian dishes ["Biryani", "Dosa", "Chaat", "Samosa", "Paneer Butter Masala"], write a program to find the index of "Samosa". If the dish is not present, the program should print "Dish not found".

```python
dishes = ["Biryani", "Dosa", "Chaat", "Samosa", "Paneer Butter Masala"]

try:

    print(dishes.index("Samosa"))  # Output: 3

except ValueError:

    print("Dish not found")
```

15.   Write a Python program to remove duplicate numbers from the list [10, 20, 30, 20, 40, 10, 50] and print the unique elements while maintaining the order.

```python
numbers = [10, 20, 30, 20, 40, 10, 50]

unique_numbers = []

for num in numbers:

    if num not in unique_numbers:

        unique_numbers.append(num)

print(unique_numbers)  # Output: [10, 20, 30, 40, 50]
```

Scenario Based Questions

Q1. Travel Itinerary Management System

You are tasked with building a travel itinerary management system for a travel agency. The system should allow the user to:

- ❖ Add destinations to a list of places they wish to visit in India.

- ❖ Modify a destination name if the user decides to change their plan.

- ❖ Remove a destination once it has been visited.

- ❖ Sort the list alphabetically for easy reference.

- ❖ Add an extra destination to the list if needed (using the insert() method).

- ❖ After the visit, print the updated list of destinations.

Example:

- ❖ The user starts with a list: ["Delhi", "Agra", "Jaipur"].

- ❖ After visiting "Agra", the user removes it and adds "Goa".

- ❖ After sorting and adding "Udaipur", the final list should be: ["Delhi", "Goa", "Jaipur", "Udaipur"].

Q2. Student Score Management System

Create a Python program for managing student scores in an exam. You need to:

- ❖ Store scores for five students in a list.

- ❖ Update a student's score if they retake the exam.

- ❖ Remove a student from the list if they drop out.

- ❖ Append the new score of a student who had missed the exam.

- ❖ Sort the scores in descending order to determine the top scorer.

- ❖ Find and print the average score of all students.

Example:

- ❖ Original scores: [88, 95, 77, 82, 65]

- ❖ After updates: Add the score 85 for a student, remove 65, and sort the remaining scores.

- ❖ Final output should include the sorted list of scores and the average score.

Q3. Library Book Tracking System

A library needs a system to track the availability of books. You are required to create:

- ❖ A list of books in the library.

- ❖ Allow staff to mark a book as borrowed or returned (modifying the list by removing or adding books).

- ❖ Generate a list of available books after some books are borrowed and others are returned.

- ❖ Sort the list of books alphabetically and print the updated list.

- ❖ Check if a specific book is available in the library by its title.

Example:

- ❖ Initial book list: ["The Alchemist", "The God of Small Things", "Pride and Prejudice"].

- ❖ After borrowing "The Alchemist", remove it from the list.

- ❖ After returning a book, reinsert it into the list and print the sorted list of available books.

Q4. **E-commerce Product List Management**

Develop a Python program for an e-commerce website to manage a list of products. The program should:

- ❖ Create an initial list of products available in stock.

- ❖ Allow adding a new product to the list and remove a product if it's no longer available.

- ❖ Update the quantity of a product in the list.

- ❖ Display all available products and their quantities.

- ❖ Use slicing to print products that are under a specific price range.

- ❖ Sort the list of products based on price.

Example:

- ❖ Product list: [("Shirt", 500), ("Pants", 700), ("Shoes", 1500)]

- ❖ After adding a new product and removing one, display the updated list and sorted products by price.

Q5. **Restaurant Order Management System**

You are building a restaurant order management system. The system should:

- ❖ Maintain a list of ordered items.

- ❖ Allow the customer to add new items to the order.

- ❖ Allow the customer to remove items from the order if they change their mind.

- ❖ Calculate the total bill after the customer finalizes the order.

- ❖ Sort the ordered items alphabetically and print them in the sorted order.

- ❖ If a customer decides to cancel the order, clear the entire list of items.

Example:

- ❖ The customer starts with an empty order list.

- ❖ They add items: ["Burger", "Pizza", "Pasta"].

- ❖ After removing "Pizza" and adding "Sandwich", calculate the total bill and display the updated sorted list.

8. Tuples

8.1 Introduction

Tuples in Python are an ordered, immutable collection of elements. Immutable means that once a tuple is created, its elements cannot be changed or modified. This characteristic distinguishes them from lists, which are mutable. Tuples are defined using parentheses (). They are often used to store related data, such as coordinates, dimensions, or a collection of items where the order is significant.

8.2 Creating Tuples

Tuples can be created in several ways:

- Using parentheses:

my_tuple = (1, 2, 3, 'a', True)

- Using the tuple() constructor:

my_list = [1, 2, 3]

my_tuple = tuple(my_list)

- Empty tuple:

empty_tuple = ()

- Single element tuple: Note the trailing comma to differentiate it from a simple expression:

single_element_tuple = (42,)

8.3 Accessing Tuple Elements

Elements in a tuple are accessed using indexing, similar to lists. Python supports both positive and negative indexing.

- Positive indexing starts from 0, where 0 is the index of the first element.

- Negative indexing starts from -1, where -1 is the index of the last element.

my_tuple = (10, 20, 30)

first_element = my_tuple[0] # Accesses the first element (10)

last_element = my_tuple[-1] # Accesses the last element (30)

Nested tuples can also be accessed using multiple indices.

8.4 Tuple Operations

- **Concatenation:** Tuples can be concatenated using the + operator to create a new tuple.

tuple1 = (1, 2)

tuple2 = (3, 4)

concatenated_tuple = tuple1 + tuple2 # (1, 2, 3, 4)

- **Repetition:** The * operator can be used to repeat the elements of a tuple.

tuple_to_repeat = (1, 2)

repeated_tuple = tuple_to_repeat * 3 # (1, 2, 1, 2, 1, 2)

- **Membership Testing:** The in and not in operators can be used to check if an element exists within a tuple.

my_tuple = (10, 20, 30)

print(20 in my_tuple) # Output: True

- **Length:** The len() function returns the number of elements in a tuple.

my_tuple = (10, 20, 30)

length = len(my_tuple) # Output: 3

- **Minimum and Maximum:** The min() and max() functions can be used to find the minimum and maximum values in a tuple of numbers.

8.5 Tuple Methods

Tuples have two main methods:

- **count():** Returns the number of occurrences of a specified value within the tuple.

my_tuple = (1, 2, 2, 3, 4, 2)

occurrences_of_2 = my_tuple.count(2) # Output: 3

- **index():** Returns the index of the first occurrence of a specified value. Raises a ValueError if the value is not found.

my_tuple = (1, 2, 3, 4, 5)

index_of_3 = my_tuple.index(3) # Output: 2

8.6 Immutability

Tuples are immutable, meaning their elements cannot be changed after creation. This has several implications:

- **Data Integrity:** Ensures that data remains unchanged, which can be crucial in certain situations.

- **Hashing:** Tuples are hashable, allowing them to be used as keys in dictionaries.

- **Performance:** Immutability can lead to performance gains in certain scenarios.

8.7 When to Use Tuples

- **Data Integrity:** When it's essential to prevent accidental modifications to data.

- **Performance:** When fast access and efficient memory usage are required.

- **Function Returns:** To return multiple values from a function.

- **Multiple Assignments:** For convenient unpacking of multiple values.

- **Dictionary Keys:** As keys in dictionaries due to their immutability.

- **Read-Only Data:** For creating collections where the data should not be modified.

8.8 Iterating Over Tuples

Tuples can be iterated over using a for loop to access each element sequentially.

my_tuple = (10, 20, 30)

for item in my_tuple:

    print(item)

8.9 Packing and Unpacking

- **Packing:** Creating a tuple from multiple values without explicitly using parentheses.

my_tuple = 10, 20, 30

- **Unpacking:** Assigning the values from a tuple to individual variables.

x, y, z = my_tuple

The number of variables must match the number of elements in the tuple.

8.10 Comparison with Lists

- **Mutability:** Lists are mutable, while tuples are immutable.

- **Syntax:** Lists use square brackets [], tuples use parentheses ().

- **Performance:** Tuples are generally faster and more memory-efficient than lists.

8.11 Check Your Logic

1. Write a Python function that takes a tuple of integers as input and returns a new tuple containing only the even numbers.

2. Given a tuple of strings, write a Python program to create a new tuple containing the lengths of each string in the original tuple.

3. Write a Python program to find the most frequent element in a given tuple of integers.

4. Write a Python function that takes two tuples as input and returns a new tuple containing only the elements that are common to both input tuples.

5. Given a tuple of words, write a Python program to create a new tuple containing only the words that start with the letter 'a'.

6. Write a Python program that takes a tuple of numbers as input and checks if it is a palindrome (reads the same forwards and backwards).

7. Debug the following Python code:

my_tuple = (1, 2, 3)

my_list = list(my_tuple)

```
my_list[0] = 10

my_tuple = tuple(my_list)

print(my_tuple)
```

The code is supposed to modify the first element of the tuple, but it will likely result in an error. Identify and correct the error.

8. Write a Python program to create a new tuple by swapping the first and last elements of a given tuple.

9. Given a tuple of integers, write a Python program to find the sum of all the elements in the tuple.

10. Write a Python function that takes a tuple of strings as input and returns a new tuple containing only the strings that are longer than a given length.

11. Debug the following Python code:

```
my_tuple = (1, 2, 3)

for i in my_tuple:

    my_tuple[i] = i * 2

print(my_tuple)
```

The code attempts to multiply each element in the tuple by 2, but it will likely result in an error. Identify and correct the error.

12. Write a Python program to determine if a given tuple of integers is sorted in ascending order.

13. Given a tuple of words, write a Python program to create a new tuple containing the words in alphabetical order.

14. Write a Python program that takes a tuple of numbers as input and returns a new tuple containing only the unique elements.

Solution

1. **Write a Python function that takes a tuple of integers as input and returns a new tuple containing only the even numbers.**

```
def even_numbers_in_tuple(input_tuple):

    """

    This function takes a tuple of integers as input and returns a new tuple

    containing only the even numbers.

    """

    even_numbers = []  # Create an empty list to store even numbers

    for number in input_tuple:

        if number % 2 == 0:
```

```python
    even_numbers.append(number)
  return tuple(even_numbers)  # Convert the list back to a tuple


# Example usage
my_tuple = (1, 2, 3, 4, 5, 6, 7, 8)
result_tuple = even_numbers_in_tuple(my_tuple)
print(result_tuple)  # Output: (2, 4, 6, 8)
```

2. Given a tuple of strings, write a Python program to create a new tuple containing the lengths of each string in the original tuple.

```python
string_tuple = ("hello", "world", "python")
lengths_tuple = tuple(len(word) for word in string_tuple)
print(lengths_tuple)  # Output: (5, 5, 6)
```

3. Write a Python program to find the most frequent element in a given tuple of integers.

```python
from collections import Counter


integer_tuple = (1, 2, 3, 2, 1, 4, 2, 1, 2)
count_dict = Counter(integer_tuple)
most_frequent_element = count_dict.most_common(1)[0][0]
print(most_frequent_element)  # Output: 2
```

4. Write a Python function that takes two tuples as input and returns a new tuple containing only the elements that are common to both input tuples.

```python
def common_elements(tuple1, tuple2):
  """

  This function takes two tuples as input and returns a new tuple

  containing only the elements that are common to both input tuples.
  """

  return tuple(set(tuple1) & set(tuple2))


tuple1 = (1, 2, 3, 4)
tuple2 = (3, 4, 5, 6)
common_elements_tuple = common_elements(tuple1, tuple2)
```

```python
print(common_elements_tuple)  # Output: (3, 4)
```

5. Given a tuple of words, write a Python program to create a new tuple containing only the words that start with the letter 'a'.

```python
word_tuple = ("apple", "banana", "avocado", "cherry", "apricot")

a_words_tuple = tuple(word for word in word_tuple if word.startswith('a'))

print(a_words_tuple)  # Output: ('apple', 'avocado', 'apricot')
```

6. Write a Python program to check if a given tuple of integers is a palindrome (reads the same forwards and backwards).

```python
integer_tuple = (1, 2, 3, 2, 1)

is_palindrome = integer_tuple == integer_tuple[::-1]  # Reverse the tuple

print(is_palindrome)  # Output: True
```

7. Debug the following Python code:

```python
my_tuple = (1, 2, 3)

my_list = list(my_tuple)  # Convert tuple to list for mutability

my_list[0] = 10

my_tuple = tuple(my_list)  # Convert modified list back to tuple

print(my_tuple)
```

Explanation: The original code attempts to modify the tuple directly, which is not allowed as tuples are immutable. The corrected code converts the tuple to a list, modifies the list, and then converts it back to a tuple.

8. Write a Python program to create a new tuple by swapping the first and last elements of a given tuple.

```python
original_tuple = (1, 2, 3, 4)

if len(original_tuple) < 2:

    swapped_tuple = original_tuple

else:

    swapped_tuple = original_tuple[-1], *original_tuple[1:-1], original_tuple[0]

print(swapped_tuple)  # Output: (4, 2, 3, 1)
```

9. Given a tuple of integers, write a Python program to find the sum of all the elements in the tuple.

```python
integer_tuple = (1, 2, 3, 4, 5)

tuple_sum = sum(integer_tuple)

print(tuple_sum)  # Output: 15
```

10. Write a Python function that takes a tuple of strings as input and returns a new tuple containing only the strings that are longer than a given length.

```python
def long_strings(string_tuple, min_length):
    """

    This function takes a tuple of strings and a minimum length as input

    and returns a new tuple containing only the strings that are longer

    than the given minimum length.

    """

    return tuple(word for word in string_tuple if len(word) > min_length)


my_tuple = ("apple", "banana", "orange", "kiwi")

result_tuple = long_strings(my_tuple, 5)

print(result_tuple)  # Output: ('banana', 'orange')
```

11. Debug the following Python code:

```python
my_tuple = (1, 2, 3)

for i in my_tuple:

    my_tuple[i] = i * 2

print(my_tuple)
```

Explanation: The error lies in trying to modify the tuple directly within the loop. Tuples are immutable. To achieve the desired result, you should create a new list and then convert it back to a tuple:

```python
my_tuple = (1, 2, 3)

new_list = [i * 2 for i in my_tuple]

new_tuple = tuple(new_list)

print(new_tuple)  # Output: (2, 4, 6)
```

12. Write a Python program to determine if a given tuple of integers is sorted in ascending order.

```python
integer_tuple = (1, 2, 3, 4, 5)

is_sorted = all(integer_tuple[i] <= integer_tuple[i+1] for i in range(len(integer_tuple)-1))

print(is_sorted)  # Output: True
```

13. Given a tuple of words, write a Python program to create a new tuple containing the words in alphabetical order.

```python
word_tuple = ("apple", "banana", "cherry")

sorted_tuple = tuple(sorted(word_tuple))

print(sorted_tuple)  # Output: ('apple', 'banana', 'cherry')
```

14. Write a Python program that takes a tuple of numbers as input and returns a new tuple containing only the unique elements.

number_tuple = (1, 2, 3, 2, 1, 4, 5, 4)

unique_tuple = tuple(set(number_tuple))

print(unique_tuple) # Output: (1, 2, 3, 4, 5)

Scenario Based Questions

1.   **Inventory Management:**

Imagine you are developing a simple inventory management system for a small store. Each item in the inventory is represented by a tuple containing the item name, quantity, and price.

a) Create a tuple containing the following inventory items:

* ("Laptop", 10, 1200) * ("Mouse", 50, 20) * ("Keyboard", 25, 80) * ("Headphones", 30, 150)

b) Write a function calculate_total_value() that takes the inventory tuple as input and calculates the total value of the entire inventory.

c) Write a function update_inventory() that takes the inventory tuple, an item name, and a new quantity as input. The function should return a new inventory tuple with the updated quantity for the specified item.

d) Write a function find_item() that takes the inventory tuple and an item name as input and returns the price of that item. If the item is not found, return None.

2.   **Student Grade Management:**

A school uses tuples to store student information, where each tuple represents a student and contains their name, roll number, and a tuple of their grades in different subjects.

a) Create a tuple of students:

* ("Alice", 1, (90, 85, 92)) * ("Bob", 2, (88, 78, 95)) * ("Charlie", 3, (75, 82, 80))

b) Write a function calculate_average_grade() that takes the student tuple as input and calculates the average grade for a given student by their roll number.

c) Write a function find_top_student() that takes the student tuple as input and returns the name of the student with the highest average grade.

d) Write a function add_student() that takes the student tuple, a new student name, roll number, and a tuple of their grades, and returns a new student tuple with the added student.

3.   **Game Development - High Scores (Advanced)**

In a complex arcade game, players can achieve multiple scores within a single session. High scores are now stored as a tuple of tuples, where each inner tuple represents a player and contains their name, a list of their scores, and their best score.

a) Create a high score tuple with the following players:

* ("Player1", [1500, 1200, 1800], 1800)

* ("Player2", [1200, 1550, 1100], 1550)

* ("Player3", [950, 1000, 1150], 1150)

b) Write a function add_new_score() that takes the high score tuple, a player name, and their new score as input. * If the player exists, update their list of scores and recalculate their best score. * If the player does not exist, add a new tuple for the player with their name, a list containing the new score, and the new score as their best score. * If the new score is higher than the current best score for that player, update the best score. * Return the updated high score tuple.

c) Write a function find_top_three() that takes the high score tuple as input and returns a new tuple containing the top three players based on their best scores.

d) Write a function calculate_player_average() that takes the high score tuple and a player name as input and calculates the average score for that player across all their recorded games.

4.   **Data Analysis - Temperature Records (Advanced)**

A sophisticated weather station records temperature readings every hour throughout the day. Temperature records are stored as a tuple of tuples, where each inner tuple represents a day and contains the date (as a string), a list of hourly temperature readings (floats), and the average temperature for that day.

a) Create a temperature record tuple with the following data for three days:

* ("2024-07-01", [28.5, 29.0, 29.5, 30.0, 29.2, 28.8, 27.5, 28.0, 28.5, 29.0, 29.5, 30.0], 29.0)

* ("2024-07-02", [30.2, 30.5, 31.0, 30.8, 30.5, 30.2, 29.8, 30.0, 30.5, 31.0, 30.8, 30.5], 30.4)

* ("2024-07-03", [29.8, 30.0, 29.5, 29.2, 29.0, 28.8, 28.5, 29.0, 29.5, 30.0, 29.5, 29.2], 29.2)

b) Write a function find_hottest_hour() that takes the temperature record tuple as input and returns the date and hour of the hottest temperature recorded across all days.

c) Write a function calculate_daily_temperature_range() that takes the temperature record tuple as input and returns a new tuple containing the date and the temperature range (maximum - minimum) for each day.

d) Write a function detect_temperature_trends() that analyzes the temperature records and attempts to identify any significant trends (e.g., increasing temperatures, decreasing temperatures, periods of consistent temperatures) and returns a descriptive string summarizing the findings.

9. Sets In Python

9.1 Introduction to Sets

Sets in Python are unordered collections of unique elements. Unlike lists or tuples, sets do not allow duplicate values, and their elements are not stored in a specific order.

Characteristics of sets include:

- **Unique Elements**: Each element in a set must be unique. Duplicate values are automatically removed.

- **Unordered**: Sets do not maintain the order of elements, and their position can change each time they are accessed.

- **Mutable**: While the elements of a set must be immutable, the set itself can be modified (elements can be added or removed).

- **Unindexed**: Sets do not support indexing or slicing, unlike lists or tuples.

For example:

languages = {"Hindi", "English", "Tamil", "Hindi"}

print(languages)

Output: {'Hindi', 'English', 'Tamil'} (duplicates are removed)

9.2 Creating Sets

Sets can be created using curly braces {} or the set() constructor.

Using Curly Braces:
Elements of a set are placed inside curly braces.

states = {"Maharashtra", "Kerala", "Punjab"}

print(states)

Output: {'Maharashtra', 'Kerala', 'Punjab'}

Using set() Constructor:
This is useful when converting other iterables (like lists, tuples, or strings) into a set.

From a list

cities = set(["Mumbai", "Delhi", "Chennai"])

print(cities)

Output: {'Mumbai', 'Delhi', 'Chennai'}

From a string

chars = set("Namaste")

```python
print(chars)
# Output: {'N', 'a', 'm', 's', 't', 'e'}
```

9.3 Adding Elements to a Set

The add() method allows adding single elements to a set.

```python
fruits = {"Mango", "Banana"}

fruits.add("Guava")

print(fruits)

# Output: {'Guava', 'Mango', 'Banana'}
```

Adding duplicate elements has no effect:

```python
fruits.add("Mango")

print(fruits)

# Output: {'Guava', 'Mango', 'Banana'}
```

9.4 Removing Elements from a Set

Elements can be removed using remove(), discard(), or pop().

Using remove(): Raises an error if the element is not found.

```python
states = {"Gujarat", "Rajasthan", "Karnataka"}

states.remove("Rajasthan")

print(states)

# Output: {'Gujarat', 'Karnataka'}
```

Using discard(): Does not raise an error if the element is not found.

```python
states.discard("Punjab")

print(states)

# Output: {'Gujarat', 'Karnataka'}
```

Using pop(): Removes and returns an arbitrary element.

```python
removed_state = states.pop()

print(removed_state)

print(states)

# Output: 'Gujarat'

# Remaining: {'Karnataka'}
```

9.5 Set Operations

Python sets support various mathematical operations such as union, intersection, and difference.

Union: Combines all unique elements from both sets.

```
set1 = {"Mumbai", "Pune"}

set2 = {"Delhi", "Mumbai"}

print(set1 | set2)

# Output: {'Mumbai', 'Pune', 'Delhi'}
```

Intersection: Retains only the common elements.

```
print(set1 & set2)

# Output: {'Mumbai'}
```

Difference: Retains elements in the first set but not in the second.

```
print(set1 - set2)

# Output: {'Pune'}
```

Symmetric Difference: Retains elements that are unique to each set.

```
print(set1 ^ set2)

# Output: {'Pune', 'Delhi'}
```

9.6 Set Methods

Python provides various built-in methods for set operations.

- union(): Combines all unique elements.
- intersection(): Finds common elements.
- difference(): Retains elements of one set not in another.
- symmetric_difference(): Finds unique elements from both sets.
- issubset(): Checks if a set is a subset of another.
- issuperset(): Checks if a set is a superset of another.

9.7 Frozen Sets

Frozen sets are immutable versions of sets. They are created using the frozenset() constructor.

```
frozen_states = frozenset(["Tamil Nadu", "Andhra Pradesh"])

# frozen_states.add("Kerala")  # Raises AttributeError
```

9.8 Use Cases for Sets

- **Removing Duplicates**:

numbers = [10, 20, 20, 30]

unique_numbers = set(numbers)

print(unique_numbers)

Output: {10, 20, 30}

- **Membership Testing**:

states = {"Maharashtra", "Gujarat", "Goa"}

print("Goa" in states)

Output: True

- **Finding Common Data**:

tags1 = {"python", "coding"}

tags2 = {"coding", "data"}

print(tags1 & tags2)

Output: {'coding'}

- **Mathematical Operations**: Efficient for set theory tasks in computational problems.

9.9 Performance and Limitations

- **Performance**: Sets use hash tables, making membership testing and modifications highly efficient (average $O(1)$ time complexity).

- **Limitations**: Sets are unordered, do not support indexing, and require elements to be hashable (immutable).

Sets in Python are a versatile and efficient data structure, useful for a variety of real-world applications, especially those involving uniqueness and membership testing. Examples rooted in the Indian context help relate these concepts to practical scenarios.

9.10 Check Your Logic

1. Create a set of all vowels in the English alphabet. Given an input string, write a program to find which vowels are missing from the input string and print them as a set.

2. Write a Python program to check whether two given sets are disjoint. If they are not, find and print their intersection.

3. You are given two sets representing users who like Bollywood and Hollywood movies. Write a program to find the users who like only Bollywood movies, only Hollywood movies, and both types of movies.

4. Debug the following code and correct the errors to remove duplicate numbers from a list and print the unique numbers:

numbers = [1, 2, 2, 3, 4, 5, 3, 6]

unique_numbers = numbers.unique()

print(unique_numbers)

5. Write a program to simulate a cricket match scoreboard. Create a set of players who have scored more than 50 runs and another set for players with more than 5 wickets. Find players who appear in both sets and print their names.

6. Given a list of Indian cities, write a program to find and print the cities that start with vowels. Ensure that the solution does not include duplicate city names.

7. Create a set of integers and write a program to determine if all numbers in the set are prime. If not, print the non-prime numbers.

8. Debug the following program that aims to find the symmetric difference between two sets of employee IDs:

set1 = {101, 102, 103, 104}

set2 = [103, 104, 105, 106]

diff = set1 ^ set2

print(diff)

9. You are given sets of students enrolled in different courses at an Indian university. Write a Python program to determine:
a) Students enrolled in all courses.
b) Students enrolled in at least one course.
c) Students enrolled in exactly two courses.

10. Debug the following program that intends to find the union of two sets:

set_a = {"apple", "banana"}

set_b = {"cherry", "banana"}

union_set = set_a.add(set_b)

print(union_set)

11. Write a program to remove the stop words from a given paragraph. Use a set of predefined stop words to filter out common words, leaving only unique and meaningful words.

12. You are given two sets: one representing Indian festival names and another representing holidays. Write a program to determine:

a) Festivals that are holidays.

b) Festivals that are not holidays.

13. Create a Python program to generate all possible subsets of a given set and print them. For example, given the set {1, 2, 3}, the output should include {}, {1}, {2}, {3}, {1, 2}, {1, 3}, {2, 3}, {1, 2, 3}.

14. Debug the following code that intends to copy a set and update the copied set with new elements without modifying the original set:

fruits = {"mango", "apple"}

copied_fruits = fruits

copied_fruits.update(["orange", "banana"])

print(fruits)

print(copied_fruits)

15. Write a program to find the difference between two sets of temperatures recorded in different Indian cities during summer and winter. Ensure that the program handles negative temperatures appropriately and prints the cities with significant temperature differences.

Solutions

1. Missing Vowels from Input String

vowels = {'a', 'e', 'i', 'o', 'u'}

input_string = "education"

present_vowels = set(input_string.lower()) & vowels

missing_vowels = vowels - present_vowels

print("Missing vowels:", missing_vowels)

Output: Missing vowels: {'u'}

2. Check for Disjoint Sets

set1 = {1, 3, 5}

set2 = {2, 4, 6}

if set1.isdisjoint(set2):

    print("The sets are disjoint.")

else:

    print("Common elements:", set1 & set2)

Output: The sets are disjoint.

3. Analyze Movie Preferences

bollywood = {"Rahul", "Priya", "Anjali"}

```python
hollywood = {"Anjali", "Sam", "David"}

only_bollywood = bollywood - hollywood

only_hollywood = hollywood - bollywood

both = bollywood & hollywood

print("Only Bollywood:", only_bollywood)

print("Only Hollywood:", only_hollywood)

print("Both:", both)

# Output: Only Bollywood: {'Rahul', 'Priya'}

#        Only Hollywood: {'Sam', 'David'}

#        Both: {'Anjali'}
```

4. Debugging Duplicate Removal

Corrected Code:

```python
numbers = [1, 2, 2, 3, 4, 5, 3, 6]

unique_numbers = set(numbers)

print(unique_numbers)

# Output: {1, 2, 3, 4, 5, 6}
```

5. Cricket Match Scoreboard

```python
more_than_50_runs = {"Virat", "Rohit", "KL Rahul"}

more_than_5_wickets = {"Jadeja", "Ashwin", "KL Rahul"}

both = more_than_50_runs & more_than_5_wickets

print("Players in both categories:", both)

# Output: Players in both categories: {'KL Rahul'}
```

6. Cities Starting with Vowels

```python
cities = ["Agra", "Mumbai", "Indore", "Ahmedabad", "Delhi", "Udaipur"]

vowels = {'A', 'E', 'I', 'O', 'U'}

result = {city for city in cities if city[0].upper() in vowels}

print("Cities starting with vowels:", result)

# Output: Cities starting with vowels: {'Ahmedabad', 'Agra', 'Indore', 'Udaipur'}
```

7. Check for Prime Numbers in a Set

```python
def is_prime(num):
```

```python
    if num < 2:
        return False
    for i in range(2, int(num**0.5) + 1):
        if num % i == 0:
            return False
    return True


numbers = {11, 13, 17, 18, 20}
non_primes = {num for num in numbers if not is_prime(num)}
print("Non-prime numbers:", non_primes)
# Output: Non-prime numbers: {18, 20}
```

8. Debugging Symmetric Difference

Corrected Code:

```python
set1 = {101, 102, 103, 104}
set2 = {103, 104, 105, 106}
diff = set1 ^ set2
print(diff)
# Output: {101, 102, 105, 106}
```

9. Course Enrollment Analysis

```python
course1 = {"Aarav", "Ananya", "Rohan"}
course2 = {"Ananya", "Rohan", "Sanya"}
course3 = {"Aarav", "Sanya"}
all_courses = course1 & course2 & course3
at_least_one = course1 | course2 | course3
exactly_two = (course1 & course2 | course2 & course3 | course1 & course3) - all_courses
print("All courses:", all_courses)
print("At least one course:", at_least_one)
print("Exactly two courses:", exactly_two)
# Output: All courses: set()
#         At least one course: {'Aarav', 'Ananya', 'Rohan', 'Sanya'}
```

```
#        Exactly two courses: {'Ananya', 'Rohan'}
```

10. Debugging Union of Sets

Corrected Code:

```
set_a = {"apple", "banana"}

set_b = {"cherry", "banana"}

union_set = set_a | set_b

print(union_set)

# Output: {'apple', 'banana', 'cherry'}
```

11. Removing Stop Words

```
text = "Python programming is fun and useful for many applications"

stop_words = {"is", "and", "for"}

words = set(text.lower().split())

filtered_words = words - stop_words

print("Filtered words:", filtered_words)

# Output: Filtered words: {'python', 'many', 'programming', 'useful', 'applications'}
```

12. Festivals and Holidays

```
festivals = {"Diwali", "Holi", "Eid", "Pongal"}

holidays = {"Holi", "Eid", "Christmas"}

both = festivals & holidays

not_holidays = festivals - holidays

print("Festivals that are holidays:", both)

print("Festivals that are not holidays:", not_holidays)

# Output: Festivals that are holidays: {'Holi', 'Eid'}

#        Festivals that are not holidays: {'Diwali', 'Pongal'}
```

13. Generating Subsets of a Set

```
from itertools import chain, combinations

def all_subsets(s):

    return chain(*map(lambda x: combinations(s, x), range(0, len(s)+1)))

s = {1, 2, 3}

subsets = list(all_subsets(s))
```

```python
print("Subsets:", subsets)
# Output: Subsets: [(), (1,), (2,), (3,), (1, 2), (1, 3), (2, 3), (1, 2, 3)]
```

14. Debugging Set Copy and Update

Corrected Code:

```python
fruits = {"mango", "apple"}
copied_fruits = fruits.copy()
copied_fruits.update(["orange", "banana"])
print("Original set:", fruits)
print("Updated set:", copied_fruits)
# Output: Original set: {'mango', 'apple'}
#         Updated set: {'mango', 'apple', 'orange', 'banana'}
```

15. Temperature Difference

```python
summer = {"Delhi": 42, "Mumbai": 34, "Chennai": 37}
winter = {"Delhi": 12, "Mumbai": 21, "Chennai": 24}
temp_diff = {city: summer[city] - winter[city] for city in summer if city in winter}
print("Temperature differences:", temp_diff)
# Output: Temperature differences: {'Delhi': 30, 'Mumbai': 13, 'Chennai': 13}
```

Scenario Based Questions

1. Festival Attendance Analysis

A cultural organization tracks attendance at various Indian festivals. The attendance is recorded as sets of names for each festival.

    a)   Find and print the names of attendees who participated in all the festivals.

    b)   Identify the names of attendees who participated in exactly one festival.

    c)   Allow the program to add a new attendee to a specific festival while ensuring no duplicates.

Example:

```python
festival1 = {"Aarav", "Riya", "Priya"}
festival2 = {"Riya", "Aman", "Priya", "Neha"}
festival3 = {"Priya", "Rohan", "Aarav"}
```

Expected Output:

Attendees in all festivals: {"Priya"}

Attendees in only one festival: {"Aman", "Neha", "Rohan"}

After adding "Sanya" to festival1: {"Aarav", "Riya", "Priya", "Sanya"}

2. Cricket Tournament Analysis

During a cricket tournament, the sets of players who scored above 50 runs and players who took more than 3 wickets are recorded.

a) Find and print the names of players who achieved both milestones.

b) List all players who achieved at least one milestone.

c) Remove a player from both sets if they have retired and print the updated sets.

Example:

run_scorers = {"Virat", "Rohit", "Rahul", "Dhoni"}

wicket_takers = {"Ashwin", "Jadeja", "Rahul", "Shami"}

Expected Output:

Players achieving both: {"Rahul"}

Players achieving at least one: {"Virat", "Rohit", "Rahul", "Dhoni", "Ashwin", "Jadeja", "Shami"}

After removing "Rahul": {"Virat", "Rohit", "Dhoni"} and {"Ashwin", "Jadeja", "Shami"}

3. Movie Preference Analysis

An entertainment survey collects the preferences of participants for different genres of movies.

a) Identify participants who like all genres (Action, Drama, and Comedy).

b) Find participants who like only one genre.

c) Add a new participant to all genres and print the updated sets.

Example:

action_lovers = {"Aarav", "Riya", "Karan"}

drama_lovers = {"Karan", "Riya", "Neha"}

comedy_lovers = {"Riya", "Neha", "Priya"}

Expected Output:

Participants who like all genres: {"Riya"}

Participants who like only one genre: {"Aarav", "Priya"}

After adding "Sanya":

- Action lovers: {"Aarav", "Riya", "Karan", "Sanya"}

- Drama lovers: {"Karan", "Riya", "Neha", "Sanya"}

- Comedy lovers: {"Riya", "Neha", "Priya", "Sanya"}

4. Team Selection for Sports Events

A school is selecting students for two sports teams: cricket and football.

a) Identify students who are selected for both teams.

b) Find students who are selected for only one team.

c) Allow the addition of a new student to any team, ensuring no duplicates.

Example:

cricket_team = {"Ananya", "Rohan", "Aarav"}

football_team = {"Rohan", "Sanya", "Aarav"}

Expected Output:

Students in both teams: {"Rohan", "Aarav"}

Students in only one team: {"Ananya", "Sanya"}

After adding "Kunal" to cricket_team: {"Ananya", "Rohan", "Aarav", "Kunal"}

5. Library Membership Analysis

A library tracks its members based on their preferences for fiction and non-fiction books.

a) Find and print the names of members who borrow books from both categories.

b) Identify members who borrow books from exactly one category.

c) Remove a member from both sets if their membership expires and print the updated sets.

Example:

fiction_members = {"Priya", "Karan", "Neha"}

non_fiction_members = {"Karan", "Rahul", "Neha"}

Expected Output:

Members in both categories: {"Karan", "Neha"}

Members in exactly one category: {"Priya", "Rahul"}

After removing "Karan":

- Fiction members: {"Priya", "Neha"}

- Non-fiction members: {"Rahul", "Neha"}

10. Dictionaries In Python

10.1 Creating Dictionaries

Dictionaries in Python are unordered collections of data stored as key-value pairs. Each key within a dictionary must be unique and immutable (e.g., strings, numbers, tuples).

10.1.1 Using Curly Braces {}

This is the most common way to create a dictionary.

my_dict = {'name': 'Alice', 'age': 30, 'city': 'New York'}

10.1.2 Using the dict() Constructor

You can create a dictionary using the dict() constructor with keyword arguments:

my_dict = dict(name='Alice', age=30, city='New York')

10.1.3 From a List of Tuples

Create a dictionary from a list of tuples, where each tuple represents a key-value pair:

pairs = [('name', 'Alice'), ('age', 30), ('city', 'New York')]

my_dict = dict(pairs)

10.1.4 Dictionary Comprehension

Create dictionaries dynamically using concise syntax:

squares = {x: x**2 for x in range(1, 6)} # Dictionary of squares

10.1.5 Using zip() Function

Create a dictionary from two lists, one for keys and one for values:

keys = ['name', 'age', 'city']

values = ['Alice', 30, 'New York']

my_dict = dict(zip(keys, values))

10.2 Accessing Elements in a Dictionary

10.2.1 Using Square Brackets []

Access values by using the corresponding key within square brackets:

my_dict = {'name': 'Alice', 'age': 30}

print(my_dict['name']) # Output: Alice

- **KeyError:** Raises a KeyError if the key does not exist.

10.2.2 Using the get() Method

Access values safely with the get() method. It returns None if the key is not found, or an optional default value:

print(my_dict.get('age')) # Output: 30

print(my_dict.get('city', 'Unknown')) # Output: Unknown (default value)

10.3 Modifying Dictionaries

10.3.1 Changing Existing Values

Change the value associated with a key:

my_dict['age'] = 31

10.3.2 Adding New Items

Add a new key-value pair to the dictionary:

my_dict['city'] = 'New York'

10.3.3 Removing Items

- Use del to remove an item:

del my_dict['age']

- Use pop() to remove and return the value:

value = my_dict.pop('city')

10.3.4 Removing All Items

Use the clear() method to remove all key-value pairs:

my_dict.clear()

10.4 Dictionary Methods

Python dictionaries come with a variety of built-in methods to perform common operations, making it easier to manipulate and manage dictionary data.

a. keys()

The keys() method returns a view object that displays all the keys in the dictionary. A view object reflects changes made to the dictionary, meaning that if you modify the dictionary, the view will automatically reflect these changes.

Example:

my_dict = {'name': 'Alice', 'age': 30, 'city': 'New York'}

keys = my_dict.keys()

print(keys) # Output: dict_keys(['name', 'age', 'city'])

Here, keys() provides a view object that contains all the keys in the dictionary.

b. values()

The values() method returns a view object that displays all the values in the dictionary. Like keys(), the values() method returns a view that is updated when the dictionary is modified.

Example:

my_dict = {'name': 'Alice', 'age': 30, 'city': 'New York'}

values = my_dict.values()

print(values) # Output: dict_values(['Alice', 30, 'New York'])

In this example, values() returns a view object containing all the dictionary values.

c. items()

The items() method returns a view object that contains all the key-value pairs in the dictionary as tuples. Each tuple contains a key and its associated value.

Example:

my_dict = {'name': 'Alice', 'age': 30, 'city': 'New York'}

items = my_dict.items()

print(items) # Output: dict_items([('name', 'Alice'), ('age', 30), ('city', 'New York')])

This method returns a view object of key-value pairs, where each pair is represented as a tuple.

d. update()

The update() method is used to update a dictionary with the key-value pairs from another dictionary or an iterable of key-value pairs. If a key already exists, the value is updated; otherwise, a new key-value pair is added.

Example:

my_dict = {'name': 'Alice', 'age': 30}

other_dict = {'city': 'New York', 'age': 31}

my_dict.update(other_dict)

print(my_dict) # Output: {'name': 'Alice', 'age': 31, 'city': 'New York'}

In this example, the age key is updated with the value 31, and the city key is added from other_dict.

e. pop()

The pop() method removes the specified key and returns its associated value. If the key is not found, a KeyError is raised. Optionally, you can provide a default value to return if the key is not found.

Example:

my_dict = {'name': 'Alice', 'age': 30, 'city': 'New York'}

value = my_dict.pop('age')

print(value) # Output: 30

print(my_dict) # Output: {'name': 'Alice', 'city': 'New York'}

Here, pop() removes the key 'age' and returns its value 30.

f. popitem()

The popitem() method removes and returns an arbitrary key-value pair from the dictionary as a tuple. This method is typically used to remove and retrieve the last inserted key-value pair in versions of Python before 3.7, but in newer versions, it removes an arbitrary item.

Example:

my_dict = {'name': 'Alice', 'age': 30, 'city': 'New York'}

item = my_dict.popitem()

print(item) # Output: ('city', 'New York')

print(my_dict) # Output: {'name': 'Alice', 'age': 30}

This method removes and returns a random item as a tuple. In this example, it removes the 'city' key-value pair.

g. clear()

The clear() method removes all items from the dictionary, effectively making it an empty dictionary.

Example:

my_dict = {'name': 'Alice', 'age': 30, 'city': 'New York'}

my_dict.clear()

print(my_dict) # Output: {}

The clear() method empties the dictionary, removing all key-value pairs.

10.5 Dictionary Comprehensions

Basic Comprehension: Create a dictionary concisely:

squares = {x: x**2 for x in range(1, 6)}

Conditional Comprehension: Create a dictionary with a condition:

even_squares = {x: x**2 for x in range(1, 11) if x % 2 == 0}

Using Functions: Use functions within the comprehension:

def cube(x):

    return x**3

cubes = {x: cube(x) for x in range(1, 6)}

Nested Comprehension: Create nested dictionaries:

nested_dict = {x: {y: x*y for y in range(1, 4)} for x in range(1, 4)}

10.6 Nesting Dictionaries

Create dictionaries within dictionaries to represent hierarchical data:

people = {

   'person1': {'name': 'Alice', 'age': 30},

   'person2': {'name': 'Bob', 'age': 25}

}

10.7 Dictionary Operations

10.7.1 Checking Key Existence

To check if a key exists in a dictionary, you can use the in keyword. This allows you to test for the presence of a key, and if it exists, you can retrieve its value using the get() method. If the key does not exist, get() can return a default value.

Example:

my_dict = {'name': 'Alice', 'age': 30, 'city': 'New York'}

if 'name' in my_dict:

   value = my_dict.get('name', 'Not Found')

   print(value) # Output: Alice

In this example, we first check if the key 'name' exists in the dictionary using in. If it does, we use the get() method to retrieve its value.

10.7.2 Getting Length

To get the number of items (key-value pairs) in a dictionary, you can use the len() function. This function returns the total count of key-value pairs.

Example:

my_dict = {'name': 'Alice', 'age': 30, 'city': 'New York'}

length = len(my_dict)

print(length) # Output: 3

Here, len(my_dict) returns the number of items in the dictionary.

10.7.3 Iterating Over a Dictionary

You can iterate over a dictionary in several ways:

1. Iterating over keys using for key in my_dict.

2. Iterating over values using for value in my_dict.values().

3. Iterating over key-value pairs using for key, value in my_dict.items().

Example:

my_dict = {'name': 'Alice', 'age': 30, 'city': 'New York'}

Iterating over keys

for key in my_dict:

   print(key)

Output: name, age, city

Iterating over values

for value in my_dict.values():

   print(value)

Output: Alice, 30, New York

Iterating over key-value pairs

for key, value in my_dict.items():

   print(f"{key}: {value}")

Output: name: Alice, age: 30, city: New York

In this example, we demonstrate three different ways to iterate over a dictionary, depending on whether you need to access keys, values, or both.

10.8 Immutable Keys

Dictionary keys in Python must be **immutable**. This means that they cannot be changed after they are created. Common immutable types include strings, numbers, and tuples. On the other hand, **mutable** objects like lists or sets cannot be used as dictionary keys because their contents can change, which would interfere with the dictionary's internal hashing mechanism.

Example of valid dictionary keys:

my_dict = {('name', 'first'): 'Alice', 1: 'one', 'age': 30}

In this example, the tuple ('name', 'first'), the integer 1, and the string 'age' are valid keys because they are immutable.

Example of invalid dictionary keys:

```python
my_dict = {[1, 2, 3]: 'List Key'}  # Raises TypeError
```

Here, trying to use a list as a dictionary key raises a TypeError because lists are mutable.

10.9 Use Cases for Dictionaries

Dictionaries are versatile data structures in Python with a wide range of practical applications. They are commonly used in situations where efficient data retrieval and mapping are needed. Below are some of the key use cases for dictionaries:

1. **Efficient Data Storage and Retrieval**
   Dictionaries allow quick access to data via unique keys, making them ideal for storing and retrieving data efficiently.

2. **Mapping Relationships Between Items**
   Dictionaries are perfect for representing relationships, such as mapping a person's name to their phone number, or a student's ID to their grades.

3. **Handling Configuration Settings**
   Storing configuration settings in a dictionary enables easy access and modification of values based on predefined keys, such as a settings file for an application.

4. **Counting Occurrences of Items**
   Dictionaries can be used to count occurrences of elements (such as words in a text) by using the element as the key and its count as the value.

5. **Grouping Data by Key**
   When data needs to be grouped under a common identifier, dictionaries provide an easy way to group related items using a key. For example, grouping employees by department.

6. **Caching Results**
   Dictionaries are often used to implement caching mechanisms, storing computed results that can be quickly retrieved instead of recalculating them.

7. **Representing JSON Data**
   Since JSON data is typically represented as key-value pairs, dictionaries are a natural choice for storing and manipulating JSON-like data structures.

8. **Implementing Switch-Case Logic**
   While Python does not have a built-in switch-case statement, dictionaries can be used to simulate this logic by mapping cases to functions or actions.

9. **Tracking Inventory**
   Dictionaries are useful for tracking inventory in a store, where product names or IDs are the keys and their quantities are the corresponding values.

10. **Simulating Data Structures (Graphs, Trees)**
    Dictionaries are often used to represent more complex data structures like graphs or trees, where nodes are represented by keys and edges or child nodes are stored as values.

10.10 Check Your Logic

1. Create a dictionary to store the names of five cities in India and their respective populations. Write a program that takes a city name as input and prints the corresponding population.

2. You are given a dictionary where keys are product names and values are their prices in INR. Write a program to find the most expensive product.

3. A dictionary contains the names of students as keys and their marks as values. Write a program to find the student with the highest marks.

4. Create a dictionary with the names of states in India as keys and their capitals as values. Write a program that takes a state name as input and returns the capital.

5. Debug the following code to correctly store and display a list of students who passed in an exam. The dictionary should store the student's name as the key and a boolean indicating whether they passed or failed as the value:

students = {'Amit': 'pass', 'Rajesh': 'fail', 'Sunita': True}

print(students)

6. You have a dictionary with the names of employees in a company as keys and their salaries as values. Write a program that increases the salary of all employees by 10%.

7. Create a dictionary where the keys are movie titles and the values are the release years. Write a program to print all movies released after 2010.

8. Write a program that takes a list of strings containing names of Indian fruits and returns a dictionary where the fruit name is the key and the length of the name is the value.

9. Debug the following code so it correctly adds new values to the existing dictionary of favorite dishes and their types:

fav_dishes = {'Pani Puri': 'Snack'}

fav_dishes['Sambar'] = 'Main Course'

print(fav_dishes)

10. Given a dictionary containing the names of books and the number of pages, write a program that finds and prints the book with the maximum number of pages.

11. Write a program that takes a list of cities in India and returns a dictionary where the key is the city name and the value is its respective population. Use the appropriate values for these cities: Mumbai, Delhi, Kolkata, Chennai, and Bangalore.

12. You are given a dictionary where the keys are departments in a company and the values are the list of employees in those departments. Write a program that displays all the employees in the "Marketing" department.

13. Debug the following code to fix the error in accessing the value for a key that does not exist in the dictionary:

employee_data = {'name': 'Raj', 'position': 'Manager'}

print(employee_data['salary'])

14. Create a dictionary where the keys are course names (like "Math", "Science", "History") and the values are the names of students enrolled in each course. Write a program to print all the students enrolled in "Science".

15. You have a dictionary that contains the names of products and their quantities in stock. Write a program to check if a product is out of stock and display the appropriate message.

Solution

City Population Lookup

Create a dictionary with city names as keys and populations as values. Use the .get() method for input-based lookups.

cities = {'Mumbai': 12442373, 'Delhi': 11007835}

city_name = input("Enter city name: ")

print(cities.get(city_name, "City not found"))

2. Most Expensive Product

Use the max() function with key=products.get to find the most expensive product.

products = {'Laptop': 45000, 'Smartphone': 25000}

most_expensive = max(products, key=products.get)

print(most_expensive)

3. Student with Highest Marks

Find the maximum value in the dictionary using max().

students = {'Amit': 85, 'Rajesh': 92}

top_student = max(students, key=students.get)

print(top_student)

4. Capital Lookup

Create a dictionary with states and their capitals. Use input to retrieve the capital.

states = {'Maharashtra': 'Mumbai', 'Delhi': 'New Delhi'}

state_name = input("Enter state name: ")

print(states.get(state_name, "State not found"))

5. Student Pass Status

Fix the dictionary with boolean values and print the status.

students = {'Amit': True, 'Rajesh': False}

```
print(students)
```

6. Salary Increase

Iterate over the dictionary and increase each employee's salary by 10%.

```
salaries = {'Rajesh': 50000}

for emp in salaries:

    salaries[emp] *= 1.10

print(salaries)
```

7. Movies Released After 2010

Filter movies based on the release year.

```
movies = {'Dangal': 2016, 'PK': 2014}

for movie, year in movies.items():

    if year > 2010:

        print(movie)
```

8. Fruit Name Length

Create a dictionary with fruit names as keys and their lengths as values.

```
fruits = ['Mango', 'Banana']

fruit_length = {fruit: len(fruit) for fruit in fruits}

print(fruit_length)
```

9. Add New Dishes

Add new key-value pairs to the dictionary.

```
fav_dishes = {'Pani Puri': 'Snack'}

fav_dishes['Sambar'] = 'Main Course'

print(fav_dishes)
```

10. Book with Maximum Pages

Use max() to find the book with the most pages.

```
books = {'Ramayana': 500, 'Mahabharata': 1200}

max_pages_book = max(books, key=books.get)

print(max_pages_book)
```

11. City Population Dictionary

Use zip() to create a dictionary from two lists (cities and populations).

```python
cities = ['Mumbai', 'Delhi']
```

```python
populations = [12442373, 11007835]
```

```python
city_population = dict(zip(cities, populations))
```

```python
print(city_population)
```

12. Get Students Enrolled in a Course

Create a dictionary with courses as keys and student lists as values.

```python
courses = {'Math': ['Amit'], 'Science': ['Rajesh']}
```

```python
print(courses['Science'])
```

13. Accessing Non-Existent Key

Fix error using get() with a default value.

```python
employee_data = {'name': 'Raj'}
```

```python
print(employee_data.get('salary', 'Salary not found'))
```

14. Print Students in a Course

Use the dictionary to access and print enrolled students.

```python
courses = {'Math': ['Amit'], 'Science': ['Rajesh']}
```

```python
print(courses['Science'])
```

15. Check If Product is Out of Stock

Check if a product exists in the inventory and display its status.

```python
inventory = {'Laptop': 5, 'Phone': 0}
product = 'Phone'
if inventory.get(product, 0) == 0:
    print(f"{product} is out of stock.")
else:
    print(f"{product} is available.")
```

Scenario Based Questions

1. University Course Enrollment System

A university tracks the enrollment of students in various courses. The system uses dictionaries to manage the students' records and their enrolled courses. Each course is represented by a key, and the value is a list of students enrolled in that course. The system needs to perform the following tasks:

a) Write a function that takes the course name as input and returns a list of all students enrolled in that course. If the course does not exist, return an appropriate message.

b) Add a new student to a specific course, ensuring that there are no duplicate enrollments.

c) Identify students who are enrolled in all the available courses and print their names.

d) Write a function that takes a student's name as input and returns a list of all courses the student is enrolled in. If the student is not enrolled in any course, print an appropriate message.

Input:

courses = {

    'Mathematics': ['Alice', 'Bob', 'Charlie'],

    'Physics': ['Alice', 'David'],

    'Chemistry': ['Bob', 'David']

}

2. Inventory Management System

You are tasked with developing an inventory management system for a retail store. The store tracks items in its inventory using a dictionary, where the keys are product names and the values are the quantities in stock. The system must support the following operations:

a) Add new products to the inventory with their quantities, ensuring that no duplicate product names are added. If a product already exists, update its quantity by adding the new stock to the existing stock.

b) Remove products from the inventory, reducing their quantities by the specified amount. If the product is not in the inventory, print an appropriate message.

c) Implement a function that returns the total number of products in stock.

d) Write a function that checks if a product is out of stock and prints a message accordingly.

Input:

inventory = {

    'Laptop': 50,

    'Smartphone': 30,

    'Tablet': 20

}

3. Employee Salary Management System

You are working on an employee salary management system for a company. The system tracks employees' salaries using a dictionary where the keys are employee names and the values are their respective salaries. The system needs to perform the following operations:

a) Write a program to update the salary of an employee by a given percentage. The employee's name and the percentage increase should be passed as inputs.

b) Calculate and print the total salary expenditure of the company.

c) Write a function that returns the name of the employee with the highest salary.

d) Write a program that removes an employee from the dictionary if they have left the company, and prints the updated employee list.

Input:

employees = {

   'Raj': 55000,

   'Amit': 45000,

   'Neha': 60000,

   'Sonia': 50000

}

4. Student Grades Tracker

A school is tracking students' grades for multiple subjects. The grades are stored in a dictionary where the keys are student names and the values are another dictionary containing subject names as keys and the corresponding grades as values. The system needs to perform the following tasks:

a) Write a function that takes a student's name as input and returns the student's average grade across all subjects.

b) Write a function that updates the grade of a student in a specific subject. If the subject does not exist for that student, add the subject and the grade.

c) Write a function that prints the name of the student with the highest average grade.

d) Write a program to list all students who have scored more than 80 in a given subject, such as "Mathematics".

Input:

grades = {

   'Alice': {'Mathematics': 85, 'Science': 90, 'History': 78},

   'Bob': {'Mathematics': 88, 'Science': 80, 'History': 85},

   'Charlie': {'Mathematics': 75, 'Science': 85, 'History': 88}

}

11. Exception Handling

11.1 Introduction to Exceptions

Exceptions in Python are unexpected events or errors that disrupt the normal flow of a program. These can occur due to invalid input, file not found, division by zero, or other runtime issues.

Key Concepts:

- **Error Types**: Python categorizes errors like SyntaxError, TypeError, ValueError, FileNotFoundError, etc., each representing a specific problem.

- **Exception Handling**: try-except blocks allow programs to catch and handle exceptions gracefully.

- **Normal Flow**: The uninterrupted sequence of instructions executed in a program.

- **Abnormal Flow**: A deviation caused by runtime errors or exceptions.

Example:

```python
try:
    number = int(input("Enter a number: "))
    print(10 / number)
except ZeroDivisionError:
    print("You cannot divide by zero!")
except ValueError:
    print("Invalid input! Please enter a number.")
```

11.2 Error Types in Python

1. **Syntax Errors**: Occur during compilation when code violates Python's syntax rules.

```python
# Example of Syntax Error
print("Hello World"  # Missing closing parenthesis
```

2. **Runtime Errors (Exceptions)**: Occur during execution, such as ZeroDivisionError or FileNotFoundError.

```python
# Example of Runtime Error
result = 10 / 0  # Raises ZeroDivisionError
```

11.3 Basic Exception Handling

Python uses try, except, else, and finally to manage exceptions.

- **try Block**: Contains code that may raise an exception.

- **except Block**: Handles specific exceptions.
- **else Block**: Executes if no exception occurs.
- **finally Block**: Always executes, used for cleanup.

Example:

```python
try:
    num = int(input("Enter a number: "))
    print(f"Square: {num**2}")
except ValueError:
    print("Please enter a valid number.")
else:
    print("No exceptions occurred.")
finally:
    print("Execution complete.")
```

11.4 Handling Specific Exceptions

Catching specific exceptions allows for targeted error management.

```python
try:
    with open("file.txt", "r") as file:
        content = file.read()
except FileNotFoundError:
    print("The file was not found.")
except IOError as e:
    print(f"Error reading file: {e}")
```

11.5 Handling Multiple Exceptions

Python allows multiple exceptions to be handled in a single block or separate blocks.

Example:

```python
try:
    num = int(input("Enter a number: "))
    print(10 / num)
except (ValueError, ZeroDivisionError) as e:
```

```
print(f"Error: {e}")
```

11.6 else and finally Blocks

- **else Block**: Runs when no exception occurs.

- **finally Block**: Always runs, typically used for cleanup.

Example:

```
try:
    num = int(input("Enter a number: "))
    print(10 / num)
except ZeroDivisionError:
    print("Cannot divide by zero.")
else:
    print("Operation successful.")
finally:
    print("Exiting program.")
```

11.7 Raising Exceptions

The raise statement triggers exceptions manually.

1. **Raising Built-in Exceptions**:

```
def divide(a, b):
    if b == 0:
        raise ZeroDivisionError("Division by zero is not allowed.")
    return a / b
print(divide(10, 2))
```

2. **Raising Custom Exceptions**:

```
class NegativeNumberError(Exception):
    def __init__(self, message):
        super().__init__(message)


def check_positive(number):
    if number < 0:
```

```
        raise NegativeNumberError("Number must be positive.")
    return number

print(check_positive(-5))
```

11.8 Custom Exceptions

Custom exceptions are defined by inheriting from the Exception class.

Example:

```
class InvalidAgeError(Exception):
    def __init__(self, age):
        self.age = age
        super().__init__(f"Invalid age: {age}. Age must be >= 18.")


try:
    age = int(input("Enter your age: "))
    if age < 18:
        raise InvalidAgeError(age)
except InvalidAgeError as e:
    print(e)
```

11.9 Exception Propagation

Unhandled exceptions propagate up the call stack, enabling centralized error handling.

Example:

```
def func1():
    return 10 / 0


def func2():
    return func1()


try:
    func2()
except ZeroDivisionError:
```

print("Caught ZeroDivisionError from a propagated exception.")

11.10 Best Practices

- Be specific in handling exceptions.

- Use finally for resource cleanup.

- Log exceptions for debugging.

- Design custom exceptions for application-specific errors.

Example:

```
try:

    num = int(input("Enter a number: "))

    print(10 / num)

except ValueError:

    print("Invalid number.")

except ZeroDivisionError:

    print("Cannot divide by zero.")

else:

    print("Successful operation.")

finally:

    print("End of program.")
```

11.11 Check Your Logic

1. Write a program to handle division by zero using a try-except block.

2. Write a program to handle invalid input when converting a string to an integer.

3. Create a program that checks if a file exists before attempting to read it.

4. Handle multiple exceptions (ValueError and ZeroDivisionError) in a single except block.

5. Use an else block to print a success message if no exceptions occur.

6. Implement a finally block to close a file even if an exception occurs.

7. Write a program that raises a ValueError for negative numbers entered by the user.

8. Define and raise a custom exception for invalid email formats.

9. Write a function that handles exceptions and returns a default value in case of an error.

10. Re-raise an exception after catching and logging it.

11. Create a nested try-except block to handle different types of exceptions in separate scopes.

12. Write a program that propagates an exception up the call stack and handles it in the main function.

Solutions:

1. Handle Division by Zero

```python
try:
    result = 10 / 0
except ZeroDivisionError:
    print("Cannot divide by zero.")
```

2. Handle Invalid Input

```python
try:
    num = int(input("Enter a number: "))
    print(f"Square: {num ** 2}")
except ValueError:
    print("Invalid input! Please enter an integer.")
```

3. Check File Existence

```python
try:
    with open("example.txt", "r") as file:
        print(file.read())
except FileNotFoundError:
    print("File not found!")
```

4. Handle Multiple Exceptions

```python
try:
    num = int(input("Enter a number: "))
    print(10 / num)
except (ValueError, ZeroDivisionError) as e:
    print(f"Error: {e}")
```

5. Use Else Block

```
try:
    result = 10 / 2
except ZeroDivisionError:
    print("Cannot divide by zero.")
else:
    print(f"Result is {result}.")
```

6. Use Finally Block

```
try:
    file = open("example.txt", "r")
    print(file.read())
except FileNotFoundError:
    print("File not found!")
finally:
    if 'file' in locals() and not file.closed:
        file.close()
    print("File closed.")
```

7. Raise ValueError

```
number = int(input("Enter a number: "))
if number < 0:
    raise ValueError("Negative numbers are not allowed.")
```

8. Custom Exception for Email Format

```
class InvalidEmailError(Exception):
    pass
email = input("Enter your email: ")
if "@" not in email:
    raise InvalidEmailError("Invalid email format.")
```

9. Handle Exception with Default Value

```python
def safe_divide(a, b):
    try:
        return a / b
    except ZeroDivisionError:
        return 0


print(safe_divide(10, 0))
```

10. Re-Raise Exception

```python
try:
    num = int("abc")
except ValueError as e:
    print(f"Caught an exception: {e}")
    raise
```

11. Nested Try-Except

```python
try:
    try:
        num = int(input("Enter a number: "))
        print(10 / num)
    except ZeroDivisionError:
        print("Cannot divide by zero.")
except ValueError:
    print("Invalid input!")
```

12. Exception Propagation

```python
def divide(a, b):
    return a / b
```

```
try:

    print(divide(10, 0))

except ZeroDivisionError:

    print("Error: Division by zero.")
```

Scenario Based Question

Note: Some questions may require knowledge of Object-Oriented Programming (OOP) concepts in Python, which will be introduced in the next unit.

1. Library Management System

A library management system tracks the books borrowed by members. Write a Python program using dictionaries where:

a. Each member's name is a key, and their borrowed books are a list of values.

b. Implement a function to borrow a book. If the book is already borrowed by another member, raise a custom exception BookAlreadyBorrowedError.

c. Implement a function to return a book. If the book is not found in the borrowed list of the member, handle the error gracefully.

d. Implement a feature to display all borrowed books and their borrowers. If no books are borrowed, print an appropriate message.

2. Flight Booking System

A flight booking system keeps track of seats available for each flight. The program should:

a. Use a dictionary where the flight number is the key, and the value is the number of seats available.

b. Allow users to book a seat. If no seats are available, raise a custom exception NoSeatsAvailableError.

c. Allow users to cancel a booking, increasing the number of available seats. If the user tries to cancel a non-existent booking, handle the error with an appropriate message.

d. Implement a function to display the available seats for all flights. If no flights exist, print an appropriate message.

3. Online Exam Portal

An online exam portal manages students' scores. Write a Python program to handle the following:

a. Store students' names as keys and their scores as values in a dictionary.

b. Write a function to update a student's score. If the student's name is not found, raise a custom exception StudentNotFoundError.

c. Write a function to calculate and display the average score of all students. Handle division by zero if no students are enrolled.

d.   Write a function to find and display the top scorer. If multiple students have the highest score, display all their names.

4. E-commerce Order System

An e-commerce platform manages orders for different customers. Implement a program where:

a.   Each customer's name is a key, and their orders (a list of items) are the values in a dictionary.

b.   Write a function to add an item to a customer's order. If the customer does not exist, raise a custom exception CustomerNotFoundError.

c.   Write a function to remove an item from a customer's order. If the item is not found, handle the exception gracefully.

d.   Write a function to calculate the total number of items ordered across all customers. Handle the case where no orders exist with an appropriate message.

12. Object Oriented Programming Concepts

12.1 Introduction

Object-Oriented Programming (OOP) is a paradigm that models real-world entities using objects, encapsulating both data (attributes) and behavior (methods). Python, as an object-oriented language, enables programmers to create structured and reusable code by employing the principles of OOP: **Encapsulation**, **Abstraction**, **Inheritance**, and **Polymorphism**.

12.2 OOP Principles

1. **Encapsulation**
   Encapsulation bundles data (attributes) and methods into a single class and restricts access to certain components to maintain control over the internal state.
   Example:

```python
class BankAccount:

    def __init__(self, account_holder, balance):

        self.__account_holder = account_holder  # Private attribute

        self.__balance = balance  # Private attribute


    def deposit(self, amount):

        self.__balance += amount

        return f"Deposited ₹{amount}. New Balance: ₹{self.__balance}"


    def get_balance(self):

        return f"Balance: ₹{self.__balance}"


# Usage

account = BankAccount("Ramesh", 5000)

print(account.deposit(2000))  # Output: Deposited ₹2000. New Balance: ₹7000
```

2. **Abstraction**
   Abstraction hides complex details and exposes only the essential features to the user.
   Example:

```python
from abc import ABC, abstractmethod
```

```python
class Payment(ABC):

    @abstractmethod

    def process_payment(self):

        pass


class UPI(Payment):

    def process_payment(self):

        return "Payment processed using UPI."


# Usage

payment_method = UPI()

print(payment_method.process_payment())  # Output: Payment processed using UPI.
```

3. **Inheritance**
   Inheritance enables a class (child) to inherit attributes and methods from another class (parent).
   Example:

```python
class Vehicle:

    def __init__(self, make, model):

        self.make = make

        self.model = model


class Car(Vehicle):

    def car_type(self):

        return f"{self.make} {self.model} is a sedan."


# Usage

car = Car("Tata", "Altroz")

print(car.car_type())  # Output: Tata Altroz is a sedan.
```

4. **Polymorphism**
   Polymorphism allows methods in different classes to have the same name but behave differently.
   Example:

```python
class Festival:

    def celebrate(self):
```

```python
    return "Celebrating the festival."

class Diwali(Festival):
    def celebrate(self):
        return "Lighting diyas for Diwali."

class Holi(Festival):
    def celebrate(self):
        return "Playing with colors for Holi."

# Usage
festival = [Diwali(), Holi()]
for f in festival:
    print(f.celebrate())
```

12.3 Classes and Objects in Python

Classes are blueprints for creating objects, while objects are specific instances of classes.
Example:

```python
class Student:
    def __init__(self, name, roll_no):
        self.name = name
        self.roll_no = roll_no

    def display_info(self):
        return f"Name: {self.name}, Roll No: {self.roll_no}"

# Usage
student1 = Student("Priya", 101)
print(student1.display_info())  # Output: Name: Priya, Roll No: 101
```

12.4 Special Methods in Python

Special methods like __init__, __str__, and __add__ allow customization of class behavior.

1. **Constructor (__init__)**
   Automatically initializes objects.
   Example:

```
class Book:

  def __init__(self, title, author):

    self.title = title

    self.author = author


book = Book("Wings of Fire", "A.P.J. Abdul Kalam")

print(f"{book.title} by {book.author}")
```

2. **String Representation (__str__)**
   Provides a user-friendly string representation of an object.
   Example:

```
class Person:

  def __init__(self, name, age):

    self.name = name

    self.age = age


  def __str__(self):

    return f"{self.name}, {self.age} years old"


person = Person("Ravi", 28)

print(person)
```

3. **Operator Overloading (__add__)**
   Customizes behavior of operators for class objects.
   Example:

```
class Time:

  def __init__(self, hours, minutes):

    self.hours = hours

    self.minutes = minutes
```

```python
def __add__(self, other):
    total_minutes = self.minutes + other.minutes
    extra_hour = total_minutes // 60
    return Time(self.hours + other.hours + extra_hour, total_minutes % 60)


def display(self):
    return f"{self.hours} hours and {self.minutes} minutes"


t1 = Time(1, 45)
t2 = Time(2, 30)
t3 = t1 + t2
print(t3.display())
```

12.5 Abstract Classes

Abstract classes cannot be instantiated and must be inherited.
Example:

```python
from abc import ABC, abstractmethod


class Vehicle(ABC):
    @abstractmethod
    def max_speed(self):
        pass


class Bike(Vehicle):
    def max_speed(self):
        return "Max speed is 120 km/h."


bike = Bike()
print(bike.max_speed())  # Output: Max speed is 120 km/h.
```

12.6 Types of Inheritance

1. **Single Inheritance:** One child class inherits from one parent class.

2. **Multilevel Inheritance:** A chain of inheritance.

3. **Multiple Inheritance:** One child class inherits from multiple parent classes.

4. **Hierarchical Inheritance:** Multiple child classes inherit from a single parent class.

Example:

```python
class Parent:
    def family_name(self):
        return "Sharma"


class Child(Parent):
    def first_name(self):
        return "Aryan"


child = Child()
print(f"{child.first_name()} {child.family_name()}")
```

12.6 Leraning by Examples

1. Encapsulation Example

```python
class Account:
    def __init__(self, account_number, balance):
        self.__account_number = account_number  # Private
        self.__balance = balance  # Private


    def deposit(self, amount):
        if amount > 0:
            self.__balance += amount
            return f"Deposited ₹{amount}. Current balance: ₹{self.__balance}"
        return "Invalid amount"
```

```python
def get_balance(self):

    return f"Current balance: ₹{self.__balance}"


account = Account("123456789", 5000)

print(account.deposit(2000))  # Output: Deposited ₹2000. Current balance: ₹7000

print(account.get_balance())  # Output: Current balance: ₹7000
```

2. Abstraction Example

```python
from abc import ABC, abstractmethod


class Appliance(ABC):

    @abstractmethod

    def switch_on(self):

        pass


class Fan(Appliance):

    def switch_on(self):

        return "The fan is now spinning."


class Light(Appliance):

    def switch_on(self):

        return "The light is now glowing."


fan = Fan()

light = Light()

print(fan.switch_on())  # Output: The fan is now spinning.

print(light.switch_on())  # Output: The light is now glowing.
```

3. Inheritance Example

```python
class Vehicle:
```

```python
    def __init__(self, make, model):
        self.make = make
        self.model = model


class Car(Vehicle):
    def details(self):
        return f"This car is a {self.make} {self.model}."


car = Car("Tata", "Altroz")
print(car.details())  # Output: This car is a Tata Altroz.
```

4. Polymorphism Example

```python
class Shape:
    def area(self):
        pass


class Circle(Shape):
    def __init__(self, radius):
        self.radius = radius

    def area(self):
        return 3.14 * self.radius ** 2


class Square(Shape):
    def __init__(self, side):
        self.side = side

    def area(self):
        return self.side * self.side
```

```python
shapes = [Circle(7), Square(4)]
for shape in shapes:
    print(f"Area: {shape.area()}")  # Output: Area of Circle and Square
```

5. Class and Object Example

```python
class Student:
    def __init__(self, name, roll_no):
        self.name = name
        self.roll_no = roll_no

    def introduce(self):
        return f"I am {self.name}, roll number {self.roll_no}."


student = Student("Rohan", 21)
print(student.introduce())  # Output: I am Rohan, roll number 21.
```

6. Special Methods Example

```python
class Product:
    def __init__(self, name, price):
        self.name = name
        self.price = price

    def __str__(self):
        return f"Product: {self.name}, Price: ₹{self.price}"

    def __add__(self, other):
        return self.price + other.price


item1 = Product("Laptop", 50000)
item2 = Product("Phone", 20000)
```

```python
print(item1)  # Output: Product: Laptop, Price: ₹50000
print(f"Total Cost: ₹{item1 + item2}")  # Output: Total Cost: ₹70000
```

7. Abstract Class Example

```python
from abc import ABC, abstractmethod


class Payment(ABC):
    @abstractmethod
    def process_payment(self):
        pass


class UPI(Payment):
    def process_payment(self):
        return "UPI payment processed."


class Card(Payment):
    def process_payment(self):
        return "Card payment processed."


payment_method = UPI()
print(payment_method.process_payment())  # Output: UPI payment processed.
```

8. Types of Inheritance Examples

Single Inheritance

```python
class Parent:
    def display(self):
        return "This is a parent class."


class Child(Parent):
    pass
```

```python
child = Child()

print(child.display())  # Output: This is a parent class.
```

Multilevel Inheritance

```python
class Grandparent:

    def message(self):

        return "Grandparent says hello."


class Parent(Grandparent):

    pass


class Child(Parent):

    pass


child = Child()

print(child.message())  # Output: Grandparent says hello.
```

Multiple Inheritance

```python
class Parent1:

    def method1(self):

        return "This is Parent1."


class Parent2:

    def method2(self):

        return "This is Parent2."


class Child(Parent1, Parent2):

    pass


child = Child()

print(child.method1())  # Output: This is Parent1.
```

print(child.method2()) # Output: This is Parent2.

12.7 Check your Logic

1. Create a class Employee with attributes name, age, and salary. Add a method display_info() that displays the employee's details. Create an object of the class and display its information.

Solution:

```python
class Employee:
    def __init__(self, name, age, salary):
        self.name = name
        self.age = age
        self.salary = salary

    def display_info(self):
        return f"Name: {self.name}, Age: {self.age}, Salary: ₹{self.salary}"


# Create object
emp = Employee("Amit", 30, 50000)
print(emp.display_info())
```

2. Create a class BankAccount with methods for deposit() and withdraw(). Add validation to ensure that a withdrawal cannot exceed the balance.

Solution:

```python
class BankAccount:
    def __init__(self, holder_name, balance):
        self.holder_name = holder_name
        self.balance = balance

    def deposit(self, amount):
        self.balance += amount
        return f"Deposited ₹{amount}. Current balance: ₹{self.balance}"
```

```python
    def withdraw(self, amount):
        if amount > self.balance:
            return "Insufficient balance."
        self.balance -= amount
        return f"Withdrew ₹{amount}. Current balance: ₹{self.balance}"


# Create object
account = BankAccount("Ravi", 10000)
print(account.deposit(5000))
print(account.withdraw(12000))  # Insufficient balance
```

3. Create a class Person with an attribute name. Create a method greet() to print a greeting message. Inherit this class in a Student class and add an attribute roll_no.

Solution:

```python
class Person:
    def __init__(self, name):
        self.name = name

    def greet(self):
        return f"Hello, {self.name}!"


class Student(Person):
    def __init__(self, name, roll_no):
        super().__init__(name)
        self.roll_no = roll_no


# Create object
student = Student("Raj", 101)
print(student.greet())  # Output: Hello, Raj!
```

4. Demonstrate polymorphism by creating a Shape class with a method area(). Inherit this class to create a Circle and Rectangle class, overriding the area() method.

Solution:

```python
class Shape:

    def area(self):

        pass


class Circle(Shape):

    def __init__(self, radius):

        self.radius = radius


    def area(self):

        return 3.14 * self.radius ** 2


class Rectangle(Shape):

    def __init__(self, length, width):

        self.length = length

        self.width = width


    def area(self):

        return self.length * self.width


# Create objects

circle = Circle(5)

rectangle = Rectangle(4, 6)


print(circle.area())  # Output: 78.5

print(rectangle.area())  # Output: 24
```

5. Create a class Book with attributes title, author, and price. Define methods to set and get the price of the book. Use the __str__() method to represent the book as a string.

Solution:

```python
class Book:
    def __init__(self, title, author):
        self.title = title
        self.author = author
        self.__price = 0  # Private attribute

    def set_price(self, price):
        self.__price = price

    def get_price(self):
        return f"Price of '{self.title}' is ₹{self.__price}"

    def __str__(self):
        return f"Book: {self.title}, Author: {self.author}"


# Create object
book = Book("The Alchemist", "Paulo Coelho")
book.set_price(399)
print(book)
print(book.get_price())
```

6. Create an abstract class Vehicle with an abstract method fuel_efficiency(). Create two subclasses Car and Truck that implement this method.

Solution:

```python
from abc import ABC, abstractmethod


class Vehicle(ABC):
    @abstractmethod
    def fuel_efficiency(self):
        pass
```

```python
class Car(Vehicle):

    def fuel_efficiency(self):

        return "Car fuel efficiency: 15 km/l"


class Truck(Vehicle):

    def fuel_efficiency(self):

        return "Truck fuel efficiency: 8 km/l"


# Create objects

car = Car()

truck = Truck()

print(car.fuel_efficiency())

print(truck.fuel_efficiency())
```

7. Demonstrate multiple inheritance by creating two classes Mammal and Bird. Create a class Bat that inherits from both Mammal and Bird.

Solution:

```python
class Mammal:

    def walk(self):

        return "Mammal walks"


class Bird:

    def fly(self):

        return "Bird flies"


class Bat(Mammal, Bird):

    def sound(self):

        return "Bat makes a sound"


# Create object
```

```
bat = Bat()
print(bat.walk())  # Output: Mammal walks
print(bat.fly())   # Output: Bird flies
print(bat.sound()) # Output: Bat makes a sound
```

8. Create a class Library with a method add_book(). Add an exception handling mechanism to check if a book already exists before adding it.

Solution:

```
class BookAlreadyExistsError(Exception):

    pass


class Library:

    def __init__(self):

        self.books = []


    def add_book(self, book):

        if book in self.books:

            raise BookAlreadyExistsError(f"'{book}' already exists in the library.")

        self.books.append(book)

        return f"'{book}' added to the library."


library = Library()

print(library.add_book("Ramayana"))

print(library.add_book("Mahabharata"))

try:

    print(library.add_book("Ramayana"))

except BookAlreadyExistsError as e:

    print(e)
```

9. Create a class Student with methods to set and get the student's marks. Also, create a method average() to calculate the average marks of a student.

Solution:

```python
class Student:
    def __init__(self, name):
        self.name = name
        self.marks = []

    def set_marks(self, marks):
        self.marks = marks

    def get_marks(self):
        return self.marks

    def average(self):
        return sum(self.marks) / len(self.marks) if self.marks else 0


# Create object
student = Student("Amit")
student.set_marks([75, 80, 85, 90])
print(student.get_marks())  # Output: [75, 80, 85, 90]
print(f"Average Marks: {student.average()}")  # Output: Average Marks: 82.5
```

10. Create a class Movie with attributes name, genre, and rating. Implement a method display_details() to print movie details.

Solution:

```python
class Movie:
    def __init__(self, name, genre, rating):
        self.name = name
        self.genre = genre
        self.rating = rating

    def display_details(self):
```

```
    return f"Movie: {self.name}, Genre: {self.genre}, Rating: {self.rating}"


# Create object

movie = Movie("Sholay", "Action", 8.5)

print(movie.display_details())  # Output: Movie: Sholay, Genre: Action, Rating: 8.5
```

11. Demonstrate operator overloading by creating a class Time that allows adding two Time objects.

Solution:

```
class Time:
    def __init__(self, hours, minutes):
        self.hours = hours
        self.minutes = minutes

    def __add__(self, other):
        total_minutes = self.minutes + other.minutes
        total_hours = self.hours + other.hours + (total_minutes // 60)
        return Time(total_hours, total_minutes % 60)

    def display(self):
        return f"{self.hours} hours and {self.minutes} minutes"


# Create objects

time1 = Time(2, 30)

time2 = Time(1, 45)

time3 = time1 + time2

print(time3.display())  # Output: 4 hours and 15 minutes
```

12. Create a class Rectangle with methods area() and perimeter(). Create an object of the class and calculate the area and perimeter of the rectangle.

Solution:

```
class Rectangle:
```

```python
    def __init__(self, length, width):
        self.length = length
        self.width = width


    def area(self):
        return self.length * self.width


    def perimeter(self):
        return 2 * (self.length + self.width)


# Create object
rectangle = Rectangle(5, 3)
print(f"Area: {rectangle.area()}")  # Output: Area:
```

13. Builiding Applications

13.1 Questions

Question 1: Python Application for Student Information System

Topic: Python Basics, Data Types, Functions, Loops, Conditional Statements
Design a Python-based Student Information System with the following functionalities:

a. Implement a method to add student details, including name, roll number, marks, and grade.

b. Develop a function to display a list of all students along with their details.

c. Create a function to update the grades and marks of an existing student.

d. Design a feature to delete a student record based on the roll number.

Requirements:

- Utilize appropriate data structures (e.g., lists, dictionaries) to store and manage student data.

- Implement functions to add, view, update, and delete student records.

- Incorporate loops and conditional statements for handling user interactions.

- Handle edge cases such as invalid input using exception handling mechanisms.

Question 2: Library Management System

Topic: Object-Oriented Programming, Functions, Exception Handling, Lists, Loops
Design a Library Management System with the following functionalities:

a. Develop a function to add books to the library, including details such as title, author, genre, and availability status.

b. Implement a search feature that allows users to find books by title or author.

c. Create functionality to borrow and return books, ensuring that the availability status is updated accordingly.

d. Develop a feature to track overdue books and calculate fines based on overdue days.

Requirements:

- Implement classes for book records and library management, encapsulating relevant attributes and methods.

- Include methods within the classes to add, search, borrow, and return books.

- Handle exceptional cases such as attempting to borrow an unavailable book using appropriate exception handling.

- Use lists or dictionaries to manage book records and ensure data integrity.

- Design a user interface that allows librarians or users to interact with the system.

Question 3: E-commerce Shopping Cart System

Topic: Python Functions, Data Types (Dictionaries, Lists), String Operations, Loop Control
Design an e-commerce shopping cart system where users can perform the following operations:

a. Browse a catalog of items, each represented by a name, description, price, and stock.

b. Add items to the shopping cart and specify the quantity of each item.

c. View the contents of the shopping cart, displaying the total price of the selected items.

d. Remove items from the shopping cart.

e. Proceed to checkout, and if applicable, apply any available discounts.

Requirements:

- Use dictionaries to represent products and a list to store items added to the shopping cart.

- Implement functions for adding, removing, and viewing items in the shopping cart.

- Ensure that the system handles edge cases such as insufficient stock when adding an item.

- Use loops to allow users to interact with the cart dynamically.

- Format output using string operations to enhance the user experience.

Question 4: Personal Budget Tracker

Topic: Python Functions, Loops, Conditional Statements, Exception Handling
Develop a Python application to track personal finances. The system should allow users to:

a. Record income and expense transactions.

b. View the current balance by calculating the difference between income and expenses.

c. List all transactions, categorizing them (e.g., food, entertainment, bills).

d. Filter and display transactions by specific categories.

e. Provide a summary of the total income and expenses.

Requirements:

- Utilize functions for adding income, adding expenses, and calculating the balance.

- Implement exception handling to manage invalid input, such as non-numeric data.

- Store transaction data in dictionaries with relevant fields (type, amount, category).

- Use loops to enable users to interact with the system efficiently.

- Display a final summary of the budget in a user-friendly format.

Question 5: Student Grade Management System Using Object-Oriented Programming

Topic: Object-Oriented Programming, Classes and Objects, Methods, Exception Handling Create a Python application to manage student grades. The system should allow users to:

a. Add student information, including name, roll number, and grades for various subjects.

b. Calculate the average grade for each student based on their grades.

c. Display the grades and average for all students.

d. Update grades for existing students.

e. Determine and display the highest and lowest grades across all students.

Requirements:

- Define a Student class with attributes for name, roll number, subjects, and grades.

- Implement methods in the class to calculate the average grade and modify individual grades.

- Ensure that invalid operations, such as modifying a non-existent student's grade, are handled through exception handling.

- Store all student data in a list of Student objects.

- Provide a main menu for users to interact with the system and generate necessary reports.

13.2 Solution

Solution 1: Python Application for Student Information System

```python
# Define a student class

class Student:

    def __init__(self, name, roll_number, marks, grade):

        self.name = name

        self.roll_number = roll_number

        self.marks = marks

        self.grade = grade


    def update_grade(self, new_marks):

        self.marks = new_marks

        self.grade = self.calculate_grade()
```

```python
    def calculate_grade(self):
        if self.marks >= 90:
            return "A+"
        elif self.marks >= 80:
            return "A"
        elif self.marks >= 70:
            return "B+"
        elif self.marks >= 60:
            return "B"
        elif self.marks >= 50:
            return "C"
        else:
            return "F"


# List to store student data
students = []


# Add students
students.append(Student("Shivansh", "001", 85, "A"))
students.append(Student("Dhruvika", "002", 72, "B+"))
students.append(Student("Rohit", "003", 95, "A+"))


# Display students
def display_students():
    for student in students:
        print(f"Name: {student.name}, Roll No: {student.roll_number}, Marks: {student.marks}, Grade: {student.grade}")


# Update grade
```

```python
def update_student_marks(roll_number, new_marks):

    for student in students:

        if student.roll_number == roll_number:

            student.update_grade(new_marks)

            print(f"Updated {student.name}'s grade to {student.grade}")

            break

    else:

        print(f"Student with Roll No {roll_number} not found.")


# Delete a student

def delete_student(roll_number):

    global students

    students = [student for student in students if student.roll_number != roll_number]

    print(f"Student with Roll No {roll_number} has been deleted.")


# Example usage

display_students()

update_student_marks("002", 88)

display_students()

delete_student("003")

display_students()
```

Solution 2: Library Management System

```python
class Book:

    def __init__(self, title, author, genre, availability):

        self.title = title

        self.author = author

        self.genre = genre

        self.availability = availability
```

```python
    def borrow_book(self):
        if self.availability > 0:
            self.availability -= 1
            print(f"You have borrowed the book '{self.title}'.")
        else:
            print(f"Sorry, '{self.title}' is not available.")


    def return_book(self):
        self.availability += 1
        print(f"You have returned the book '{self.title}'.")



# Library
library = [
    Book("The Alchemist", "Paulo Coelho", "Fiction", 5),
    Book("Sapiens", "Yuval Noah Harari", "Non-fiction", 2),
    Book("Chetan Bhagat", "One Indian Girl", "Romance", 3)
]


# Search books by title or author
def search_book(query):
    for book in library:
        if query.lower() in book.title.lower() or query.lower() in book.author.lower():
            print(f"Found: {book.title} by {book.author}")
        else:
            print(f"No matches for '{query}'.")


# Example usage
search_book("Paulo Coelho")
library[0].borrow_book()
```

```
library[0].return_book()
```

Solution 3: E-commerce Shopping Cart System

```python
# Catalog of items
catalog = {
    "Shirt": {"price": 500, "stock": 10},
    "Jeans": {"price": 1200, "stock": 5},
    "Sneakers": {"price": 2500, "stock": 3},
    "Watch": {"price": 1500, "stock": 7}
}

cart = {}

# Add item to cart
def add_to_cart(item_name, quantity):
    if item_name in catalog:
        if catalog[item_name]["stock"] >= quantity:
            cart[item_name] = cart.get(item_name, 0) + quantity
            catalog[item_name]["stock"] -= quantity
            print(f"{quantity} {item_name}(s) added to your cart.")
        else:
            print(f"Sorry, not enough stock for {item_name}.")
    else:
        print(f"{item_name} is not available in the catalog.")

# View cart
def view_cart():
    total_price = 0
    for item, quantity in cart.items():
        price = catalog[item]["price"]
```

```python
        print(f"{item}: {quantity} x ₹{price} = ₹{price * quantity}")
        total_price += price * quantity
    print(f"Total: ₹{total_price}")


# Example usage
add_to_cart("Shirt", 2)
add_to_cart("Jeans", 1)
view_cart()
```

Solution 4: Personal Budget Tracker

```python
transactions = []


# Record transaction
def record_transaction(transaction_type, amount, category):
    transactions.append({"type": transaction_type, "amount": amount, "category": category})


# View balance
def view_balance():
    income = sum(t["amount"] for t in transactions if t["type"] == "income")
    expenses = sum(t["amount"] for t in transactions if t["type"] == "expense")
    print(f"Total Income: ₹{income}")
    print(f"Total Expenses: ₹{expenses}")
    print(f"Current Balance: ₹{income - expenses}")


# List transactions by category
def list_transactions_by_category(category):
    for t in transactions:
        if t["category"] == category:
            print(f"{t['type'].capitalize()} - ₹{t['amount']} for {category}")
```

```python
# Example usage
record_transaction("income", 50000, "Salary")

record_transaction("expense", 2000, "Food")

record_transaction("expense", 1500, "Entertainment")

view_balance()

list_transactions_by_category("Food")
```

Solution 5: Student Grade Management System Using Object-Oriented Programming

```python
class Student:

    def __init__(self, name, roll_number, subjects_grades):

        self.name = name

        self.roll_number = roll_number

        self.subjects_grades = subjects_grades


    def calculate_average(self):

        return sum(self.subjects_grades.values()) / len(self.subjects_grades)


    def display_grades(self):

        print(f"Grades for {self.name} (Roll No: {self.roll_number}):")

        for subject, grade in self.subjects_grades.items():

            print(f"{subject}: {grade}")


    def update_grade(self, subject, new_grade):

        self.subjects_grades[subject] = new_grade

        print(f"Updated {subject} grade to {new_grade} for {self.name}.")


# List of students
students = [

    Student("Shivansh", "001", {"Math": 85, "Science": 78, "English": 88}),

    Student("Dhruvika", "002", {"Math": 90, "Science": 92, "English": 85}),
```

```python
]

# Display student details
def display_all_students():
    for student in students:
        student.display_grades()


# Update grade
def update_student_grade(roll_number, subject, new_grade):
    for student in students:
        if student.roll_number == roll_number:
            student.update_grade(subject, new_grade)
            break
    else:
        print(f"Student with Roll No {roll_number} not found.")


# Example usage
display_all_students()
update_student_grade("001", "Math", 90)
display_all_students()
```